Religion and Euroscepticism in Brexit Britain

Religion has a significant effect on how Europeans feel about the European Union (EU) and has had an important impact on how people voted in the UK's 'Brexit referendum'. This book provides a clear and accessible quantitative study of how religion affects Euroscepticism and political behaviour.

It examines how religion has affected support for EU membership since the UK joined the European Economic Community, through to the announcement of the Brexit referendum in 2013, to the referendum itself in 2016. It also explores how religion continues to affect attitudes towards the EU post-Brexit. The volume provides valuable insights into why the UK voted to leave the EU. Furthermore, it highlights how religion affects the way that citizens throughout Europe assess the benefits, costs and values associated with EU membership, and how this may influence public opinion regarding European integration in the future.

This timely book will be of important interest to academics and students focusing on religion and public attitudes, contemporary European and British politics as well as think tanks, interest groups and those with an interest in understanding Brexit.

Ekaterina Kolpinskaya is Lecturer in British Politics at the University of Exeter, UK.

Stuart Fox is Lecturer in British Politics at Brunel University London, UK.

Routledge Focus on Religion

Religious Studies and the Goal of Interdisciplinarity
Brent Smith

Visual Thought in Russian Religious Philosophy
Pavel Florensky's Theory of the Icon
Clemena Antonova

American Babylon
Christianity and Democracy Before and After Trump
Philip S. Gorski

Avantgarde Art and Radical Material Theology
A Manifesto
Petra Carlsson Redell

Pandemic, Ecology and Theology
Perspectives on COVID-19
Edited by Alexander J. B. Hampton

Trump and History
Protestant Reactions to 'Make America Great Again'
Matthew Rowley

Theology and Climate Change
Paul Tyson

Religion and Euroscepticism in Brexit Britain
Ekaterina Kolpinskaya and Stuart Fox

For more information about this series, please visit: www.routledge.com/Routledge-Focus-on-Religion/book-series/RFR

Religion and Euroscepticism in Brexit Britain

Ekaterina Kolpinskaya
and Stuart Fox

LONDON AND NEW YORK

First published 2021
by Routledge
2 Park Square, Milton Park, Abingdon, Oxon OX14 4RN

and by Routledge
605 Third Avenue, New York, NY 10158

Routledge is an imprint of the Taylor & Francis Group, an informa business

© 2021 Ekaterina Kolpinskaya and Stuart Fox

The right of Ekaterina Kolpinskaya and Stuart Fox to be identified as authors of this work has been asserted by them in accordance with sections 77 and 78 of the Copyright, Designs and Patents Act 1988.

All rights reserved. No part of this book may be reprinted or reproduced or utilised in any form or by any electronic, mechanical, or other means, now known or hereafter invented, including photocopying and recording, or in any information storage or retrieval system, without permission in writing from the publishers.

Trademark notice: Product or corporate names may be trademarks or registered trademarks, and are used only for identification and explanation without intent to infringe.

British Library Cataloguing-in-Publication Data
A catalogue record for this book is available from the British Library

Library of Congress Cataloging-in-Publication Data
Names: Kolpinskaya, Ekaterina, author. | Fox, Stuart, author.
Title: Religion and Euroscepticism in Brexit Britain /
　Ekaterina Kolpinskaya and Stuart Fox.
Description: Abingdon, Oxon ; New York, NY : Routledge, 2021.
Identifiers: LCCN 2020057301 | ISBN 9780367342258 (hardback) |
　ISBN 9781032005621 (paperback) | ISBN 9780429324581 (ebook)
Subjects: LCSH: Religion and politics—Great Britain. | European
　Union—Great Britain. | European Union—Public opinion. | Great
　Britain—Religion. | Great Britain—Politics and government—2007– |
　European Union countries—Politics and government.
Classification: LCC BL65.P7 K65 2021 | DDC 322/.10941—dc23
LC record available at https://lccn.loc.gov/2020057301

ISBN: 978-0-367-34225-8 (hbk)
ISBN: 978-1-032-00562-1 (pbk)
ISBN: 978-0-429-32458-1 (ebk)

Typeset in Times New Roman
by Apex CoVantage, LLC

Contents

Lists of figures and tables viii
List of abbreviations x
Preface xi
Acknowledgements xiv

1 **The missing link: religion and British politics** 1

   The research questions and conclusions of the book 5
   1) What was the contribution of religion to the rise of Euroscepticism in Britain and the Brexit vote? 5
   2) How does religion affect Euroscepticism? 10
   3) How has the relationship between religion and voter behaviour in Britain changed because of rising Euroscepticism and/or Brexit? 12

2 **Theorising religion and Euroscepticism** 16

   What do we mean by 'Euroscepticism'? 16
   What do we mean by 'religion'? 17
   How does religion shape Euroscepticism? 20
     Religious belonging and Euroscepticism: the history of political and religious institutions 21
     Religious belonging and Euroscepticism: political ideology 23
     Religious belonging and Euroscepticism: religion and national identity 26
     Religious belonging and Euroscepticism: party identification 29

vi Contents

> *Religious behaviour and Euroscepticism: elite cues and social capital* 30
> *Religious belief and Euroscepticism: Christian tenets* 31
> *Conclusion* 32

3 **Euroscepticism and religion before Brexit** 33

> *Religion and the 1975 referendum* 34
> *Religion and Euroscepticism after 1975: on the road to Brexit* 42
> *The change in the relationship between religious belonging and Euroscepticism* 44
> *Conclusion* 51

4 **Religion and the Brexit referendum** 54

> *Religion and vote choice in the 2016 referendum* 57
>   *Identifying the religious effects* 62
>   *Regression analysis results* 64
> *Conclusion* 68

5 **Untangling (in)direct effects of religion on Euroscepticism** 72

> *Structural equation modelling and the relationship between religion and Euroscepticism* 74
> *The effect of religion on utilitarian and affective Euroscepticism* 75
> *Analysis details and results* 78
>   *Details of the SEMs* 78
>   *SEM results* 81
> *Summary and conclusion* 87

6 **Cushioning the blow: religion and party politics in the age of Brexit** 92

> *Religion and voting in Britain before and after Brexit* 95
>   *The origin of the 'Christian vote'* 95
>   *The 'Christian vote' and EU membership* 96
>   *A Brexit effect?* 100
> *Conclusion* 103

7 **Concluding thoughts**	106
Bibliography	111
Datasets 111	
References 112	
Index	120

Figures and tables

Figures

3.1	Vote in the 1975 referendum by religious denomination, per cent	36
3.2	Vote choice in the 1975 referendum by religiosity, per cent	39
3.3	Predicted probability of voting 'No' in the 1975 referendum by religious belonging and religiosity of childhood home, per cent	41
3.4	Eurosceptic attitudes in Britain by religious denomination, 1983–2015, per cent	45
3.5	Leave/Disapprove of the UK's membership of the EEC/EU by religious attendance, 1983–1997 and 2010–2015, per cent	48
3.6	Probability of being Eurosceptic, 1983–1997, per cent	48
3.7	Probability of being Eurosceptic, 2001–2015, per cent	49
3.8	Probability of being Eurosceptic, 2010–2015, per cent	49
4.1	Support for Brexit by religious belonging, behaviour and belief, per cent	58
4.2	Probability of supporting Brexit, per cent	64
4.3	Probability of supporting Brexit attendance and difference, per cent	65
4.4	Probability of supporting Brexit by religious attendance, per cent	67
4.5	Probability of supporting Brexit by religious belief, per cent	68
5.1	Conceptual map of Euroscepticism – regression analysis	74
5.2	Conceptual map of Euroscepticism – structural equation model analysis	75
5.3	Hypothesised relationship between religion and Euroscepticism	80
5.4	SEM results for England	81
5.5	SEM results for Scotland	82
5.6	SEM results for Wales	82
6.1	Voting behaviour of largest Christian denominations, 1979–2019 general elections, per cent	97

6.2 Electoral support of largest Christian denominations relative to wider electorate, 1979–2019 general elections, per cent 98
6.3 Change in relative support of religious voters by support for Brexit, per cent 102

Tables

1.1 Religious affiliation, attendance and the importance of religion in Britain, per cent 7
4.1 Effect of religious behaviour and belief on support for Brexit by Christian denomination, per cent 60
5.1 Total standardised effect of religion on Euroscepticism 86

Abbreviations

AES	Affective Euroscepticism
BES	British Election Study
BESIP	British Election Study Internet Panel
BNP	British National Party
EC	European Community
EU	European Union
SEM	Structural Equation Model
SNP	Scottish National Party
UES	Utilitarian Euroscepticism
UKHLS	United Kingdom Household Longitudinal Study
UKIP	United Kingdom Independence Party
WISERD	Wales Institute for Social and Economic Research and Data

Preface

While the sociology of religion is a well-established and researched field in UK academia, the study of religion in British politics is far more limited, and in contemporary research rarely moves beyond examining its association with terrorism, extremism, racism and ethnic minority studies. Research on how religion is related to British public opinion, election results, political participation or political ideology has been limited to only a handful of social scientists, such as James Tilley, Siobhan McAndrew, Ben Clements and Martin Steven. Religion is similarly afforded limited prominence in the study of Euroscepticism. Leruth, Startin and Usherwood's recently published *Routledge Handbook of Euroscepticism*, for example, is a superbly insightful, up-to-date overview of the study of one of the influential political attitudes in contemporary European politics, but makes no mention of the role of religion. Once more, research on religion in this context has largely been limited to a small number of seminal studies by scholars such as Jim Guth, Fraser Nelson, Hajo Boomgaarden, Andrew Freire and Claes de Vreese, although this is starting to change as more recent research by Sarah Hobolt, Toni Rodon, Siobhan McAndrew, Marianne Scherer and Simona Guerra adds to the debate about whether and how religion influences the way European voters feel about the European Union (EU).

The UK's Brexit referendum heralded one of the most tumultuous periods in modern British political history and presented the most substantial setback for the European project for decades. Studying Euroscepticism in Britain – and why British voters decided to leave the EU against the urging of virtually the entire political and economic elite – has become essential for anyone wishing to understand not just one of the most dramatic events in British democratic history but the nature of British politics for the foreseeable future. Yet despite the growing literature arguing that religion is a key determinant of Euroscepticism, and that it continues to exert a substantial influence on the political attitudes and behaviour of British voters, religion has (with one or two notable exceptions) been all but absent in academic studies of Brexit and its continuing influence on British politics. This also means that the opportunity to learn about the link between religion and Euroscepticism in the distinctive context of Brexit Britain has been largely overlooked.

This book helps to fill this gap; it uses more than 40 years of survey data from the British Election Study and the UK Household Longitudinal Survey to examine how religion has shaped British Euroscepticism between the referendum that confirmed the UK's membership of the European Community in 1975, the referendum that ensured its departure from the EU in 2016 and every general election in between. The result is the most detailed study of religion and Euroscepticism in Britain ever attempted, which not only helps explain why the UK became an increasingly Eurosceptic country after 1975, and why it voted to leave the EU in 2016, but also highlights the role religion played and is playing in transforming the nature of party politics in Britain. We also contribute to the growing literature on how religion shapes Euroscepticism. Most research in this field uses cross-country, cross-sectional surveys – such as the European Social Survey. While this provides breadth in terms of exploring how religion influences Euroscepticism throughout the EU, it comes at the expense of depth: analyses of *how* religion is related to Euroscepticism through its impact on other social and political characteristics are extremely difficult to sustain, and samples from any individual country are too small to enable anything but the most broad distinction between the non-religious, Protestants and Catholics. Our study instead prioritises depth, using more extensive datasets from the single national context of Britain and a number of analytic techniques to disentangle and examine the complex relationships between religion, political ideology, national identity and social capital, and to consider how those relationships vary not just between Protestants, Catholics and the non-religious, but different communities of Protestants, including Anglicans, Presbyterians, Baptists and Methodists. Throughout this book, we have presented the results of an extensive range of statistical analyses, and our discussion focuses on our conclusions and their implications rather than the details of those analyses. Readers with an interest in the full outputs of our analyses and more details of our methods can find all the information in our Supporting Information, available at: http://hdl.handle.net/10871/124138.

As we demonstrate throughout this book, the role of religion in shaping British Euroscepticism throughout its EC/EU membership has been undervalued. While not the most influential or decisive trait for explaining the Brexit vote, the religious characteristics of more than a third of British adults helped determine how they felt about EU membership and how they voted in the referendum. By far the most Eurosceptic religious community were Anglicans, a clear majority of whom voted for Brexit and provided the

Leave campaign with a large, receptive audience for their 'Take Back Control' message. At the other end of the scale were Catholics and Presbyterians, both of whom (albeit for very different reasons) were strongly opposed to Brexit. In the years before the referendum, those same religious characteristics helped push the issue of EU membership up the political agenda, helping put pressure on the Conservative Party to adopt a more Eurosceptic stance and ultimately promise the referendum that delivered Brexit. They were also transforming, and continue to transform, the historic relationships between Britain's religious communities and its major political parties. One of the starkest findings of this research is the emergence of the Conservative Party as the closest Britain has ever seen to a Christian Democratic Party, as the traditional links between Labour and the Catholic and free church Protestant communities deteriorates.

Our findings also have implications for the study of Euroscepticism outside the UK. As well as showing the effect of religion to be more complex and multi-faceted than can be identified using the methods and data typically employed to study its effect on Euroscepticism, we cast doubt on several long-standing assumptions about the relationship between the two. We argue that Catholicism is not, as frequently claimed, associated with a more pro-EU disposition, nor is Protestantism universally associated with a more Eurosceptic outlook. Instead, Catholics' greater propensity for religious participation is what leads many to support European integration, and it is *national church* Protestants that are particularly Eurosceptic while many *free church* Protestants have no distinctive views on EU membership at all.

Our research also raises many questions, not least the extent to which our findings are indeed applicable outside of the British context, why more religiously active people are less likely to be Eurosceptic, and what the emergence of the Conservative Party as Britain's answer to Germany's Christian Democratic Union will mean for the future of British party politics? Our hope is that as well as making a valuable contribution to these fields, this book provides the basis of an important and exciting agenda for future research that takes these questions beyond the context of Brexit and British politics.

Acknowledgements

We are grateful to our colleagues and mentors who have supported this research over the past four years and provided invaluable insights, advice and feedback. In particular, we would like to thank the Wales Institute for Social and Economic Research, Data and Methods (WISERD), especially Prof Chris Taylor, Prof Sally Power, Prof Ian Rees Jones and Dr Sioned Pearce. Their support for the *Young People and the EU Referendum* and *Young People and Brexit* projects led to the fielding of a YouGov survey in March 2016 that first identified a 'religious effect' during the referendum campaign, upon which our subsequent research was based. We also thank Dr Ceryn Evans, Dr Jennifer Hampton and Dr Esther Muddiman for working with us on other projects relating to religion, many insights of which have informed this study.

Since we started this project, we have presented papers at numerous conferences, seminars and workshops, and we would like to thank the organisers and participants of the *2017 Elections, Public Opinion and Parties Annual Conference, 2018 Political Studies Association Annual Conference* and the *Religion and Politics* specialist group, and *2018 WISERD Annual Conference* for their invaluable feedback and suggestions. Finally, we would like to thank Dr Siobhan McAndrew, Prof Maria Sobolewska and Dr Ben Clements, who have been a constant source of inspiration, support and motivation for this project. All errors are the responsibility of the authors' alone.

1 The missing link
Religion and British politics

> [T]his is the most dramatic and important democratic decision ever taken by the British people.
>
> Andrew Marr, 26 June 2016

If not for the date, readers could be forgiven for dismissing Andrew Marr's introduction to his Sunday programme as a regular, hyperbolic feature of any election campaign. Three days after the UK voted to leave the European Union (EU), however, it would have been difficult to find another way of describing the country's decision, as was evident in the political fallout: the Prime Minister had resigned, the Leader of the Opposition was facing a vote of no confidence, Scottish separatists were demanding another Independence Referendum, EU leaders were demanding to start Brexit negotiations and there were the first signs of a sustained increase in hate crimes targeted at migrants and minorities. The UK's withdrawal from the EU – or 'Brexit' – would dominate British politics for the next four years and herald one of the most tumultuous periods of the country's modern history, a period best described by Geoff Evans and Anand Menon as 'one of those rare moments when an advanced liberal democracy might be witnessing a profound and far-reaching political recalibration . . . [whose] impact will be felt in all parts of our country, our economy and our society' (2017: xviii).

So sudden and intense were the conflicts surrounding Brexit that one could be forgiven for thinking the 2016 referendum was their sole cause. As great a shock as Brexit was, however, it was not a bolt out of the blue but the culmination of long-running changes in voters' political values and priorities, as well as their relationships with social and political institutions (particularly political parties), that have been apparent throughout Europe for decades. Among them is the growing importance of voters' attitudes towards Europe and the EU as determinants of their priorities and voting behaviour as European integration has become more extensive and the consequences of EU membership – particularly migration – increasingly apparent in domestic politics (Leruth et al. 2018; Hobolt 2018; de Vreese et al. 2019; Evans and Menon 2017; Fieldhouse et al. 2020). While in the 1970s the consequences of EU membership were primarily felt in terms of international trade and some elements of economic policy, nowadays the EU's influence is felt in a host of domestic policy domains – from agriculture and fishing to transport, migration and climate change – as well as the local economies and communities of European citizens. As Leruth et al. (2018: 3) point out, '[n]ever in the history of European integration has there been a more salient moment to study . . . Euroscepticism', because how voters feel about European integration and institutions is now one of the most important traits to understanding and explaining European public opinion.

At the same time, the relationships that (particularly younger) Europeans develop with political and social institutions have been changing (Norris and Inglehart 2019; Fieldhouse et al. 2020; Dalton 2013). Voters are less likely to form attachments to many of the institutions that have shaped European political and social life throughout the post-war era. This includes not only political parties, but also social class, local communities and religion. British voters, for instance, are not only less likely to develop strong attachments to the Labour or Conservative Party than in previous decades, but less likely to identify as 'working-class', 'middle-class' or 'Christian' – social identities that for many underpinned their attachment to the political party with a historic role of representing that social group. There are numerous consequences of this breakdown in bonds between citizens and institutions. As well as contributing to women becoming more economically left-wing and socially liberal, and to young people being less likely to vote, it has made voters more discerning in deciding who to support in elections and more prepared to switch their support between candidates in different elections (Fieldhouse et al. 2020; Shorrocks 2018; Dalton 2013; Wattenberg 2012; Fox et al. forthcoming). Rather than voting for a party out of habit or because it represents their social group, voters are more likely to pick the party that best represents their values and interests, and to switch to another party or candidate if they are more appealing. Parties, as a result, have to work much harder to attract and retain voters' loyalty, and elections have become more unpredictable.

Brexit and the years of tumult that followed were the political consequences of how these changes manifested in the British electorate and the context of British politics. From the late 1990s, both Labour and the Conservatives focused their electoral strategies on middle class, socially liberal voters who were becoming more numerous in light of the massification of higher education, technological development and the decline of heavy industry (Ford and Goodwin 2014, 2017; Sobolewska and Ford 2020; Evans and Menon 2017). These were the voters who were least likely to identify with traditional social institutions such as class; they were also more likely to benefit from the opportunities afforded by EU membership and less opposed to the social consequences of mass migration, as well as less attached to institutions (such as churches) that could be changed or weakened by European integration. Older, working-class voters were less likely to benefit from EU membership and might even have suffered economically because of competition from EU migrants for a dwindling number of secure, well-paid low-skilled jobs. They were also more likely to be concerned about the impact of migration on the ethnic and cultural composition of their communities and their national identity, and the impact of integration on traditional markers of British culture (such as Parliament). These social conservatives were at best ignored and at worst derided by the major political parties who could nonetheless take their support for granted in elections, as long as there was no other alternative to vote for (Evans and Menon 2017; Ford and Goodwin 2017; Sobolewska and Ford 2020). Insurgent parties that put hostility to Europe, a staunch defence of traditional social values and British or English national identity, and hostility to immigration at the heart of their campaigns [such as the British National Party (BNP) and United Kingdom Independence Party (UKIP)] increasingly appealed to these voters throughout the 2000s, however, heaping pressure on the major parties to adopt more Eurosceptic stances and ultimately pushing David Cameron to promise a referendum on EU membership before the 2015 election.

The gulf between 'Remainers' and 'Leavers' in that referendum, therefore, reflected far more than differences of opinion about the benefits of EU membership: it reflected beliefs about the nature of British (or English, Welsh, Scottish or Irish) national identity; tolerance for people, values and practices from other cultures; beliefs about the benefits of social change and globalisation; views of how the UK should interact with other countries and its obligations to citizens beyond its borders; attachment to traditional social and political institutions; and beliefs about whether freedom of expression trumps one's obligations to law, order and authority. While the 2016 referendum and Brexit propelled the question of EU membership and values relating to national identity, social liberalism and conservatism, tolerance for those from other cultures and our views of globalisation to the top of the political agenda, they did not create the deep divides upon which the subsequent chaos in British politics was based. Rather, they provided the impetus for those divides to be expressed forcefully and for those on either side of them to unite around a political cause. For the same reason, any

4 *The missing link*

resolution to Brexit will not heal those divides: questions about national identity, migration, social, economic and political change, and freedom of expression versus respect for tradition and authority will continue to arise in relation to a whole host of political issues Britain and Europe will face in the future, not least how to respond to the challenge of Covid-19 and whatever relationship the UK and EU eventually forge (Sobolewska and Ford 2020). In other words, the days of Euroscepticism, Brexit and all the values, identities and beliefs associated with them being pivotal to understanding British politics are far from over.

It is to this understanding, as well as that of how and why Brexit happened and had such a dramatic effect on British politics, that our book contributes, by examining the relationship between religion and Euroscepticism in Britain. Religion is a rare feature of research on British voters, primarily because it is thought to be largely irrelevant in an increasingly secular society with religion playing limited role in public and political debate (beyond discussions of extremism, terrorism or racism) and the influence of other characteristics (age, social class and education) being more easily identifiable in social surveys. While a growing literature has questioned this omission in recent years (Tilley 2015; McAndrew 2017a, 2017b, 2020; Kolpinskaya and Fox 2019; Clements 2015), religion remains all but absent in the wealth of research on the values, identities and attitudes that underpin British Euroscepticism in the context of not only Brexit but electoral behaviour as well. This book helps fill some of this gap and sheds much-needed light on the role religion has played and will continue to play in British politics because of its relationship with Euroscepticism. Using a wealth of survey data – including panel and cross-sectional data from the British Election Study (BES) and United Kingdom Household Longitudinal Surveys (UKHLS) spanning the 40 years between the two referendums that coincided (roughly) with the duration of the UK's EU membership – we provide the most detailed study of how religion is related to British Euroscepticism ever attempted. We consider how not only religious identity but religious belief, behaviour and socialisation have been related to Euroscepticism since 1975, and how they affected voters' decisions in the 2016 referendum. We also examine the complex question of *why* religion affects Euroscepticism, that is, what it is about identifying with a religious community, engaging in religious behaviour or holding religious beliefs that make people more or less likely to be Eurosceptic? Finally, we look at how religion has affected voting behaviour in Britain since the 1970s, considering how the political loyalties of the largest religious communities have changed over time and how those religiously based loyalties have been affected by, or interacted with, the rise of new political loyalties reflecting support for or opposition to Brexit. Our research contributes not only to explanations of how and why voters made the decisions they did in the 2016

EU referendum and subsequent general elections, and to understandings of the influence of religion in contemporary British politics, but also to the wider study of Euroscepticism as an attitude that increasingly shapes public opinion and electoral events in Europe. We draw heavily on the conclusions of how religion and Euroscepticism are related in existing academic literature, but our focus on a single national context and such an extensive time period provides us with insights that allow us to move beyond, contribute to and in some cases challenge those conclusions as well.

Our book is organised around three key questions that motivated this research:

1 What was the contribution of religion to the rise of Euroscepticism in Britain and the Brexit vote?
2 How does religion affect Euroscepticism?
3 How has the relationship between religion and voter behaviour changed in Britain and has this affected or been affected by Brexit?

We summarise our findings and the answers to these questions later, with the more detailed research and discussion provided over the following five chapters. The broader implications of our research for the study of British politics on the one hand, and the future study of religion and Euroscepticism on the other, are discussed in the final chapter. Collectively, our book shows that while religion was certainly not the only or most influential characteristic to explain Brexit or the tumultuous years that followed, it did play an important and under-appreciated role in explaining why a sizeable chunk of British voters were more likely to vote 'Leave' in 2016 than we may otherwise expect. It also contributed to the rising salience of Euroscepticism as a political issue that helped put pressure on David Cameron to hold a referendum on EU membership in the first place, and the stunning victory for Boris Johnson's Conservative Party in the 2019 general election that all but confirmed that the UK would in fact leave the EU. The importance of religion to explaining and understanding Euroscepticism, therefore, means that it is vital to efforts to explain and understanding public opinion and voter behaviour in Europe and Britain for the foreseeable future.

The research questions and conclusions of the book

(1) What was the contribution of religion to the rise of Euroscepticism in Britain and the Brexit vote?

While declining church attendance and the falling number of people who identify as 'religious' in Britain has been a source of consternation among socially conservative commentators and jubilation among social liberals (e.g. Finkelstein 2017; Collins 2016), and informed the dismissal of religion as an influence on political and social attitudes in Western democracies overall (Berger 1999), many of these claims are premature. It is true that most adults in the UK do not identify with a religious community: according to the UKHLS for 2016–2018, a small majority (53 per cent) did not consider themselves to belong to any religious community. Figures for other elements of what it means to 'be religious' (which are discussed at length in Chapter 2) are similar: 51 per cent did not feel that religion made a difference to their daily lives (an indicator of how strongly one holds to religious beliefs, such as in the existence of God) while 70 per cent virtually never participated in religious services. Such data imply that religion is the pursuit of a minority – albeit a large one – in Britain. If, however, we recognise that religion is more complex than simply identifying with a religious community, and that one does not have to identify with a religious community to hold religious beliefs or participate in religious services, we find that a majority – 61 per cent – exhibit at least one religious trait. While the proportion of people in Britain who exhibit religious characteristics has indeed fallen steadily for decades (Clements 2015), when we study the potential effect of religion on political attitudes or behaviour (such as Euroscepticism), we are still looking at the potential effect of characteristics exhibited by almost two-thirds of British adults; hardly an irrelevant minority, particularly when looking at political events as close as the 52–48 per cent result of the EU referendum. Moreover, as Table 1.1 illustrates that 61 per cent are highly varied in terms of their religious identification, beliefs and behaviour. Not only could people of differing religious communities vary in their political characteristics, but there could be (and, indeed, as we show later, there are) substantial differences in how people *within* religious communities vary because of differences in their religious beliefs and behaviour. The potential for religion to be an important determinant of political characteristics, therefore, is both greater and more nuanced than a simplistic 'secularisation = less important' assumption implies.

Our examination of how the numerous facets of religion are related to Euroscepticism begins in Chapter 2, where we set out the theories for why there is a potential for religion to affect Euroscepticism at all, and what the previous literature tells us about it. We then examine how religion was related to support for membership of the European Community (EC) in the 1975 referendum in Chapter 3, as well as through the following 40 years and up to the 2016 referendum in Chapter 4. A key advantage of this work over much of the existing literature, as noted earlier, is that by focusing on the single national context of Britain we have access to more detailed survey data that cover a much longer period of time than is available to studies

Table 1.1 Religious affiliation, attendance and the importance of religion in Britain, per cent

	None	Anglican	Catholic	Pres.	Methodist	Baptist	Other Christian	Muslim	Hindu	Jewish	Sikh	Buddhist
Religion	53.0	22.6	7.7	1.9	1.8	0.8	6.4	2.5	0.9	0.4	0.4	0.3
Practically never	92 (48)	59 (13)	38 (3)	57 (1)	29 (1)	33 (0)	39 (2)	29 (1)	25 (0)	34 (0)	22 (0)	15 (0)
>Once a year	7 (4)	22 (5)	22 (2)	18 (0)	13 (0)	16 (0)	22 (1)	11 (0)	25 (0)	19 (0)	17 (0)	34 (0)
>Once a month	1 (1)	8 (2)	14 (1)	10 (0)	4 (0)	15 (0)	14 (1)	11 (0)	14 (0)	10 (0)	16 (0)	25 (0)
>Once a week	0 (0)	11 (3)	26 (2)	16 (0)	55 (0)	35 (0)	26 (2)	48 (1)	36 (0)	37 (0)	44 (0)	26 (0)
No difference	78 (41)	28 (6)	18 (1)	29 (1)	1 (0)	12 (0)	13 (1)	10 (0)	13 (0)	12 (0)	6 (0)	8 (0)
A little difference	14 (8)	28 (6)	22 (2)	25 (1)	10 (0)	20 (0)	24 (1)	11 (0)	12 (0)	18 (0)	4 (0)	11 (0)
Some difference	6 (3)	27 (6)	32 (3)	27 (1)	26 (1)	27 (0)	32 (2)	22 (0)	38 (0)	24 (0)	19 (0)	31 (0)
A great difference	2 (1)	16 (4)	28 (2)	18 (0)	57 (1)	40 (0)	30 (3)	57 (2)	37 (0)	45 (0)	71 (0)	50 (0)

Source: UKHLS. Sample weighted using UKHLS population weight and accounting for sample clustering and stratification. Figures in brackets indicate the proportion of the total sample in each category

of multiple European countries. This allows us to move beyond the simplistic categorisation of religious identity commonly used in that research, in which respondents are divided into the non-religious, Protestants and Catholics (and, occasionally, Orthodox), and examine the Euroscepticism of the five largest Christian communities in Britain. This includes the two largest national Protestant church communities – Anglicans (i.e. members of the Church of England) and Presbyterians (i.e. affiliating with and/or tracing its origin to the Church of Scotland) – members of the two largest non-national Protestant church communities (whom we refer to as 'free church Protestants') – Baptists and Methodists – and Roman Catholics. As we demonstrate repeatedly throughout this book, the distinction between national church Protestants and free church Protestants is both empirically and theoretically imperative: Baptists, Methodists, Presbyterians and Anglicans exhibit distinct attitudes towards European integration and this reflects their distinct histories, political ideologies and relationships with English, Scottish or Welsh national identities. Treating all Protestants as a single block loses a wealth of more nuanced information about how religious identity is related to Euroscepticism and leads to a mischaracterisation of the attitudes of any single Protestant community.

That said, despite our use of more extensive survey data, we are still limited to examining only the largest Christian denominations in Britain. This is partly because existing theories of religion and Euroscepticism are focused only on the effects of Christianity: the theoretical framework for how non-Christians' religious characteristics may affect their Euroscepticism is all but non-existent, and developing such a framework would require a distinct research project. Moreover, as Table 1.1 shows, most non-Christian communities in Britain are very small in number, meaning that they are barely represented in the samples of social surveys. Finding sufficient data to sustain a reliable analysis of the link between non-Christian religions and Euroscepticism is another substantial task that cannot be overcome within the scope of this project. This book also does not examine the effect of religion in Northern Ireland. While there is little doubt that religion has an important effect on Euroscepticism in Northern Ireland, the role of religion in politics there is far more prominent and complex than in Britain. To do that complexity justice would also require a distinct theoretical framework and set of analyses that are beyond the scope of this project. This book, therefore, focuses on the five largest Christian communities in Britain, who collectively make up 35 per cent of British adults. They are frequently compared with the non-religious, which constitute a further 53 per cent of British adults.

In Chapters 3 and 4, we show that as far as religious identification is concerned, the 1975 and 2016 referendums were almost mirror images of each other. In 1975, the most Eurosceptic were those of no religious identification, 34 per cent of whom voted against remaining in the EC (comparable to the national 'No' vote of 33 per cent). For the most part, Christians were more supportive of EC membership, with most Anglicans, Catholics, Presbyterians, Baptists and Methodists voting 'Yes'. Support was highest among Anglicans, three in four of whom voted 'Yes'. Over the following 40 years, however, these views were to change considerably: not only did all Christian communities become more Eurosceptic but there was also a divergence in their views, with Anglicans becoming substantially more Eurosceptic and a clear majority – 55 per cent – voting 'Leave' in 2016. The growth of Euroscepticism was more muted among the other Christian groups: Methodists and Baptists were more or less evenly divided in the 2016 referendum, while the overwhelming majority of Catholics and Presbyterians supported continued EU membership.

While the effect of religious identity on Euroscepticism changed throughout the duration of the UK's EU membership, the effects of religious behaviour and belief remained steady: both have consistently been negatively associated with Euroscepticism (though the effect of religious belief is very small), and their effects are independent of religious identity. In other words, regardless of whether the voter is Anglican, Catholic or non-religious, the more religiously active they are, the less likely they are to be Eurosceptic. This also means that the total effect of the three dimensions of religion on Euroscepticism can be complex: in some cases, they contradict each other, with some voters' religious identity associated with increased Euroscepticism (such as Anglicanism) while their behaviour is associated with a more pro-EU outlook (such as attending church every week). In other cases, they have a cumulative effect in one direction: Anglicans who virtually never attended church, for example, were more likely to vote Leave in 2016 (with 61 per cent doing so) than Anglicans who attended church every week (43 per cent of whom voted Leave). Similarly, while 39 per cent of Catholics voted for Brexit in 2016, this fell to 31 per cent among Catholics who attended church every month. Once we consider the potentially cumulative effects of the various dimensions of religion, we find that not only is religion more important than an examination of any single dimension (such as denomination) suggests, but that in a minority of cases the magnitude of that effect rivals that of characteristics more commonly associated with the differences between 'Remainers' and 'Leavers', such as age or education.

While there is no simple statistic to highlight that can summarise the answer to the question of how religion contributed to Brexit and the rise of Euroscepticism in Britain, Chapters 3 and 4 show that a sizeable minority of British voters exhibited religious characteristics that were likely to affect their support for the UK's membership of the EC/EU and how they voted in the referendums. These 'religious effects' were not constant – some increased Euroscepticism while others depressed it – and they are in some cases complex. There is little question, however, that voters' religious identification and behaviour, in particular, affected how supportive they were of EC membership in 1975; how Eurosceptic they became over the following 40 years; and how likely they were to vote for Brexit in 2016. There is no complete account of Euroscepticism during the UK's EC/EU membership that does not include the influence of British voters' religious characteristics.

(2) How does religion affect Euroscepticism?

In Chapter 5, we use the opportunity afforded by panel data (i.e. survey data collected from the same individuals repeatedly over a sustained period) to examine the complex question of why people who exhibit certain religious characteristics become more or less likely to be Eurosceptic. Specifically, we use the BES and structural equation modelling to examine how religious identification and behaviour were related to Euroscepticism during the Brexit referendum, through their impact on a host of political identities and ideological values that sit at the heart of our theories of how and why religion could shape our attitudes towards the EU. This allows us to overcome some – though not all – limitations of previous research and contribute to understandings of why people who exhibit religious characteristics are more or less likely to be Eurosceptic.

Our analyses show that, first, religious identity affects a number of deeply held political values and national identities, which in turn shape how supportive voters are of the consequences of EU membership for their communities and national social institutions, how they assess the benefits of EU membership and the performance of EU institutions, and the principle of European integration itself. The precise effects of religious identity vary, however, from one community to another. The strongest effects are found among national church Protestants: Anglicans and Presbyterians are both more likely to be socially conservative and economically right-wing, and to reject the notion of transnational European identities. They are also more likely to hold strong English and Scottish national identities, respectively, although only Englishness affects Euroscepticism. The result is that Anglicans and Presbyterians are more likely to be critical of the consequences of EU membership – particularly migration – and to perceive that the costs of EU membership for the UK outweigh the benefits. They are also not at all convinced that European integration is a worthy objective. Collectively, Anglicans and Presbyterians are the most Eurosceptic religious communities in Britain. This is perhaps surprising given that most Presbyterians voted to stay in the EU in 2016, but our analysis shows that this was a

The missing link 11

reflection of the fact that most Presbyterians lived in Scotland – the most pro-EU country in the UK. Relative to the wider, largely pro-EU Scottish electorate, Presbyterians are staunch Eurosceptics.

In stark contrast to the existing literature on religion and Euroscepticism, we find that Catholicism is similarly associated with being more socially conservative, more critical of immigration and so being more Eurosceptic. Catholics do not exhibit the same hostility towards a transnational European identity, however, nor the same attachment to an English national identity, and so their Euroscepticism is less severe than national church Protestants'. This is also surprising given that most Catholics voted against Brexit in 2016, but this is where the distinction between religious identity and behaviour is vital: while identifying as Catholic is associated with increased Euroscepticism, most Catholics are also religiously active (see Table 1.1), which depresses Euroscepticism. In other words, it is not Catholicism but regularly attending Mass that makes most Catholics supportive of the EU; religiously inactive Catholics are more likely than most to oppose EU membership.

Finally, we find that there is virtually no link between identifying with a free church Protestant community and Euroscepticism. While Baptists and Methodists tend to be slightly more socially conservative than the non-religious the difference is very small, and these communities lack the attachments to either exclusive national identities (such as English) or transnational identities (such as European) that could affect their views of the EU. Most Baptists and Methodists tend to be religiously active to some degree (as shown in Table 1.1), and this depressed their Euroscepticism in the 2016 referendum, but identifying with free church Protestant communities does not, in itself, shape one's views towards the EU. This further highlights the importance of not treating Protestants as a homogenous block.

The explanations for these effects are complex and are discussed at length in Chapter 2. What we show in Chapter 5 is that the key to understanding why religious identity makes people more or less Eurosceptic lies in, first, the ideological beliefs and values associated with those communities, and second the distinctive history of those communities – particularly their interactions with the Catholic Church and the British state – and how this shapes their political preferences today. Catholics, Anglicans and Presbyterians alike are typically more socially conservative than people who are not in those religious communities: they are wary of change, respect traditional social institutions and practices, and prioritise relationships with one's local community over global communities and obligations. This makes them less likely to view the consequences of EU membership, particularly in terms of the impact of immigration on local economies and communities, but also of European supranationalism on the power, status and identity and traditional social and political institutions, in a positive light. The history of conflict between the Catholic Church and Protestant nations, and the persecution of Protestants by the Catholic Church and its allies, also gives national church Protestants, in particular, reason to be wary of any form of European integration. These communities have relied upon a strong national state to defend them against the Catholic Church, and so anything seen to dilute or challenge that institution will be a cause for concern. The notion of a supranational authority transcending national borders is a key part of the Catholic community, on the other hand, and so European integration is less likely to arouse their concerns. If anything, constraining the power of a state infrastructure that has historically persecuted Catholics – such as the British state – could be something they welcome.

Chapter 5 also examined how religious behaviour shapes Euroscepticism, and in this regard, we surprisingly found no conclusive results at all. While there is plenty of evidence that religious behaviour depresses Euroscepticism, we could find neither tendency for more religiously active voters to be less Eurosceptic in our structural equation models (SEMs), nor any tendency for them to be more socially liberal, more tolerant of migrants or more likely to support transnational European identities. There are theories that could potentially explain why religious behaviour depresses Euroscepticism, including the influence of religious elites or the boost that religious activity brings to social capital (Smith and Woodhead 2018; McAndrew 2020; Boomgaarden and Freire 2009). Our data were unable to effectively test these and so neither can be discounted, but our analysis also raises the possibility that the effect of religious behaviour is spurious: that it is not religious behaviour but rather a trait strongly associated with religious behaviour that explains why people who go to church more often are less likely to be Eurosceptic. This is a question we are unable to resolve within the confines of this study and so identify as an important avenue for further research, which is discussed in more detail in the final chapter.

(3) How has the relationship between religion and voter behaviour in Britain changed because of rising Euroscepticism and/or Brexit?

In Chapter 6, we consider the consequences of the relationship between religion and Euroscepticism for electoral politics in Britain. Religious identity has long been associated with a tendency to support one or another political party; in fact, religion was the main social cleavage upon which the British party system was based before the 20th century. Anglicans were the basis of support for the Tory Party (which eventually became what we now know as the Conservative Party), while Catholics and so-called 'non-conformists' (i.e. free church Protestants) supported first the Whigs, then the Liberal, Labour and/or Liberal Democrat parties. The First World War and enfranchisement of the working class changed this, giving rise to political conflicts between social classes that cut across religious lines. Combined with the increasingly secularised British society and the increasing hostility exhibited by British voters towards public figures' expressing religious influence for their decisions, many have assumed that religion had no significant effect at all on voter behaviour since the Second World War (Hornsby-Smith 2015; Steven 2010; Tilley 2015). Beyond the influence of secularisation in weakening the attachments voters have to their political parties in the post-referendum era (Fieldhouse et al. 2020) the role of religion in the tumultuous period of British politics that followed the EU referendum has barely been considered.

A growing literature shows that this omission is misguided, and religious identity and behaviour, in particular, continue to shape voters' party identification and electoral decisions (Tilley 2015; McAndrew 2017a). Even voters who do not identify as members of a religious community show a preference for the party of their family's religious background, reflecting the influence of political socialisation and the intergenerational transmission of partisan beliefs from more religiously engaged parents and grandparents (Tilley 2015). In Chapter 6, we look at the voting behaviour of Britain's largest Christian communities in general elections since 1979, examining how it has changed as the processes that led to Brexit – the rise of Euroscepticism, the weakening attachments between voters and traditional social institutions, and the failure of major parties to represent socially conservative and Eurosceptic voters – shaped British elections and party politics. We also consider, however, whether the 'religious vote' has been substantially affected by the challenges to existing party loyalties posed by Brexit, or whether voters' religious characteristics shaped or mitigated how likely their party loyalties were to change in light of their Brexit preference. We know, for example, that Anglicans are more Eurosceptic than most and have a historic tendency to support the Conservative Party – so did the Conservative's shift to a staunchly pro-Brexit stance in the 2017 and 2019 elections strengthen this bond, and were Anglicans who did not vote Leave less likely to abandon the party for an anti-Brexit rival because of their historic association with the party?

Chapter 6 shows that while the size and electoral significance of the 'religious vote' have fallen as fewer people have exhibited religious characteristics, the traditional allegiances between some religious communities and political parties are still clear. Anglicans, for example, remain staunch supporters of the Conservatives, and Presbyterians also have an above-average tendency to support the party. While there have been some switches away from the Tories among Anglicans and Presbyterians opposed to Brexit, the religious link with the party acted as a buffer against such Brexit defections, that is, anti-Brexit Anglicans were less likely to switch from the Conservatives to Labour after 2015 than anti-Brexit non-Anglicans. There are also important changes underway in the 'religious vote', however, changes that – while Brexit may have accelerated them somewhat – largely precede the EU referendum and point to a more fundamental and long-running shift in the relationship between Christians and the UK's political parties. Most remarkable in this regard is the collapse of Labour's Catholic vote. Historically, Labour was *the* party of Britain's Catholic community, reflecting the party's trade union roots and the fact that most Catholics were, or were descended from, working-class migrants (primarily from Ireland) who supported the trade union movement. Since the 1980s, however, Labour's support among Catholics has steadily declined, to such an extent that, by 2019, Catholics were no more likely to support Labour than anyone else. A similar, though less pronounced, trend is the deterioration in support for Labour and the Liberal Democrats among free church Protestants, who were similarly no more likely to vote Labour in 2019 than other voters. Rather than the erosion of a partisan preference among Catholic, Baptist and Methodist communities, this reflects the replacement of their preference for Labour and/or the Liberal Democrats with a preference for the Conservatives. Conservative support amongst Catholics, Baptists and Methodists has been steadily increasing since the 1980s, and in the 2019 election, the party won marginally more support among Catholics than did Labour.

This shift in Christian support away from Labour and the Liberal Democrats to the Conservatives is the most important feature of the religious vote in British politics of the last 40 years. It was neither caused by, nor particularly strongly affected by, Brexit – but we argue that it is related to Brexit in that the same trends that led to Euroscepticism being an increasingly salient issue in the wider electorate have also contributed to this transformation of the religious vote. As we discussed earlier, the rising salience of Euroscepticism reflected not only the increasingly integrated nature of the EU but the consequences of that integration for domestic political priorities, values and identities. As Europe became more integrated so did political values such as tolerance for other cultures, views of social, economic and political change, and national identity become more important determinants of not only how voters felt about Europe but also their political priorities. Voting behaviour became increasingly shaped by voters' social conservatism or liberalism, which Chapter Five shows are strongly influenced by religion, alongside the traditional left versus right economic divide. As social conservatism and national identity became more important determinants of voters' priorities and electoral behaviour, therefore, the key influences on those values and identities – including their religion – became more important to understanding their voting behaviour and party loyalties. While there are substantial differences between denominational communities, Christian voters in general tend towards social conservatism, right-wing economic ideologies and traditional, exclusive national identities (such as Englishness). This ideological agenda aligns far more closely with the historic ideology of the Conservative Party than Labour or the Liberal Democrats, and so as voters' religious values and identities have become more important influences on their voting behaviour and party loyalty they have felt more compelled to support the Conservatives.

The uniqueness of British politics is commonly exaggerated in comparisons with other European countries, but one lasting unusual feature of the British party system is the absence of a clearly Christian political party, or a party that dominated the support of Christian communities, akin to Germany's Christian Democratic Union, Denmark's Christian Democrats or the Netherlands' Christian Union (Steven 2010). While there are considerable differences between the ideologies and policies of the Conservatives compared with those more overtly Christian parties, the most substantial change in Britain's religious vote for the last half century has seen the party emerge as the closest thing to a Christian Democratic Party the country has ever seen, and this is in large part driven by the same processes that led to Brexit.

2 Theorising religion and Euroscepticism

> At the heart of Britain's Christian heritage are certain glorious principles.... Among those principles is a vision of peace and reconciliation, of being builders of bridges, not barriers.... The vision of the founders of the European Union was also peace and reconciliation.
>
> Justin Welby, Archbishop of Canterbury, 11 June 2016

In this chapter, we set out the theoretical basis of this research, including the definition and conceptualisation of 'religion', and how its various facets are expected to be related to Euroscepticism. Drawing on an extensive literature on the nature of religion, Euroscepticism and the relationship between the two, we set out how the various dimensions of religion are expected to affect voters' support for the principle of European integration and/or their assessments of the benefits of EU membership for their country. Readers more interested in the empirical analyses and conclusions of this research will find sufficient information in the following chapters – this chapter will be of interest to those interested in the theoretical basis for the religion/Euroscepticism relationship and our interpretation of our findings, as well as the conclusions of previous literature on the subject.

What do we mean by 'Euroscepticism'?

By the time of the UK's Brexit referendum, anybody with even a passing interest in British politics will have come across the term 'Eurosceptic'. Originating in the 1980s as a way of journalists describing Conservative MPs hostile to the Single European Act, it has since become a widely used term in political campaigning, media coverage, opinion polling and academic research. At its core, the term refers to a generalised hostility towards membership of the EU or some specific element of European integration

(Taggert and Szczerbiak 2018; Leruth et al. 2018). While straight-forward, this overlooks considerable variation between different expressions of Euroscepticism and the different elements or features of integration against which they can be directed. There is a considerable difference, for example, between someone who supports the principle of European integration but feels that European institutions are failing to deliver prosperity or good government for their citizens, and someone who is opposed to the principle of integration outright, and still someone else who has no problem with the principle or the performance of European institutions but objects to the free movement of people. Each expression of Euroscepticism could be borne out of distinct values, identities and attitudes, and may even express themselves in different ways (e.g. not all of the individuals may wish to leave the EU as a result of their Euroscepticism).

Various conceptual structures of Euroscepticism have been developed to recognise and attempt to capture this depth (Sørensen 2008; Boomgaarden et al. 2011; Wessels 2007; Krowel and Abts 2007). Ideally, we would integrate such richness into our analyses and learn a lot more about religion and Euroscepticism as a result. Regardless of the conceptual and theoretical depth that can be brought to the term, however, in empirical research, we are constrained by the opportunities to represent that depth available in the data we rely on. Much of the data we use in this research comes from surveys of British voters since 1975, when surveys were more limited and difficult to gather, and the study of Euroscepticism was in its formative stages. As a result, measures of the concept were far more limited, either to expressions of support for leaving the EC or EU, or disapproval of membership. In Chapter 5, we employ a richer, multi-dimensional view that distinguishes between Euroscepticism based on principled objection to integration and that based on an assessment that the costs of EU membership outweigh the benefits. For the other chapters, however, we are forced to rely on the more limited indicators. Regardless of how it is measured, when we speak of 'Euroscepticism', we are referring to a generalised hostility to the EC/EU, the principle of European integration, or some specific element of it, that manifests itself in either dissatisfaction with EC/EU membership or support for leaving the organisation.

What do we mean by 'religion'?

When we speak of 'religion', it is easy to think of the beliefs people point to (such as in the existence of God) when stating whether or not they are religious. This is, of course, correct; belief in the existence of supernatural entities, and certain moral codes or values believed to stem from them, is a key element of religion, but it is not the only element (Bruce 2018; Clements

2015; Park and Smith 2000; Ben-Nun Bloom and Arikan 2012, 2013). Religion is a far more complex and varied institution than is often assumed, and it is vital to recognise this complexity if we are to have a hope of fully appreciating how religion could affect political attitudes or behaviour. Religion also refers, for example, to the communities (such as Anglicans or Jews) and institutions (such as churches or mosques) that people identify with. These can be the basis of forms of social identity, as well as social networks that can influence the values people express and act as a source of communal or individual resource (Caputo 2009; Fox et al. forthcoming). Association with religious beliefs, communities and institutions also implies behavioural practices. Some are associated with religious ritual or worship (such as baptism), some are the result of identification with and participation in a religious community (such as going to church), while others are the consequence of participation in religious social networks (such as taking part in activities to feed the homeless or a book group). When we talk about 'religion', therefore, it is important to remember that we are not referring to a single belief or community, but to a number of shared beliefs, values, actions, institutions and communities (Bruce 2018). It is also important to note that the expression of these different facets of religion varies between individuals. Some may hold religious beliefs (such as in the existence of God) and values (such as believing that abortion is a sin) and participate in religious activities (such as going to church) every week. Others may hold such beliefs and values without regularly going to church or interacting with religious communities. Some may believe in God but have very different beliefs about sin or right and wrong, while still others may attend church and be active in religious communities while not believing in God (Clements 2015; Davie 2015). In other words, there is not only considerable variety in the characteristics associated with religion that we must account for when studying how one's religion affects their behaviour, but there is considerable variety in the configuration of those characteristics between individuals.

There is also a generational element to the complexity with which religious characteristics can be expressed. Older people are less likely to vary in terms of their religious characteristics: identifying as a member of a religious community is likely to be accompanied by religious behaviour and beliefs consistent with the traditional expectations of that community (such as a Catholic regularly attending Mass, believing in Original Sin and in Heaven and Hell). Younger people, however, are likely to be more varied: it is far more common for them to, for example, hold certain religious beliefs (such as in God) without identifying with a religious community; to participate in religious services without holding religious beliefs; and to combine traditional elements of religion with new forms of spirituality (Vincett and Olson 2012; Wuthnow 2002, 2007; Dinham et al. 2009). Finally, different elements of religion can have different effects on social and political attitudes or behaviour (McAndrew and Voas 2011; Ben-Nun Bloom and Arikan 2012; Fox et al. forthcoming). Lam (2002), for example, shows that people who attend religious services are less likely to volunteer in their community, but identification with religious communities makes volunteering more likely. Fox et al. (forthcoming) similarly showed that older people who identify as Anglicans are likely to be less socially trusting than younger people who do so, and that participating in religious services has a positive effect on social trust while holding religious beliefs is of little importance. When we talk about 'religion', therefore, we are neither speaking about a single belief, community, practice or institution; nor a single characteristic that is expressed universally by members of society or one that has a constant effect on other characteristics – such as Euroscepticism. We are talking about a combination of identities, beliefs, practices, values and behaviours that can vary from one individual to another, that have different effects on social and political characteristics, and whose effects can vary depending on the social context and socialisation of the individual expressing them.

This presents a substantial challenge to academic research, particularly that based on survey data, such as this, because we need to use measures of 'religion' that are sufficiently sensitive to the range of communal, attitudinal and behavioural expressions it can take without losing the breadth of perspective that makes generalisations about groups of individuals possible and informative. Previous attempts to address this problem have led to scholars considering religion in terms of 'dimensions', each representing one of the major expressions of religion. The most common is a three-dimensional structure developed by Kellstedt et al. (1993) and shown by Clements (2015) to be a powerful conceptual tool for studying religion and public opinion in Britain. First is 'religious belonging', which refers to someone's identification with a religious community and the institutional framework it provides for social networks and shared beliefs (e.g. identifying as 'Catholic'). Second is 'religious behaviour', which refers to activity that expresses one's religious beliefs or is connected to one's religious community (e.g. attending religious services). Third is 'religious belief', which refers to the beliefs that one holds based on their religious values, and the strength with which they are held (e.g. belief in God). The advantage of this dimensional approach is that it allows for considerable variation to be expressed in how a given individual's religion may manifest in their social identities and networks, behaviour and beliefs, while being based on traits that are fairly easy to measure in social surveys and being straightforward enough so as to be informative. Throughout this book, we use this three-dimensional approach wherever possible, examining how religious belonging, behaviour and belief are related to Euroscepticism and voting behaviour.

How does religion shape Euroscepticism?

> There are many historical, ideological, and institutional reasons to suspect that religious factors influence public attitudes towards integration.
>
> (Nelsen et al. 2011: 2–3)

Despite being almost absent from studies of British Euroscepticism, the notion that religion might affect how European citizens feel about integration is not new. Since the early 2000s, interest in the relationship between them has grown, developed in seminal studies such as Nelsen et al. (2001), Nelsen and Guth (2003), Minkenberg (2009), Boomgaarden and Freire (2009) (see also de Vreese et al. 2009 for a discussion, and Nelsen and Guth 2015 for a more recent and detailed study). Some – such as Boomgaarden and Freire (2009) and Hobolt et al. (2011) – argue that religion does not affect Euroscepticism at all, and that the association between the two reflects confounding characteristics related to both (such as attitudes towards immigration) that scholars frequently do not account for in their analyses. Most research, however, argues that religious characteristics do affect attitudes towards European integration and that these relationships are more or less constant throughout EU Member States. The common positions of such research are:

- Catholics are the most supportive of European integration, and people living in traditionally Catholic and/or majority Catholic countries (such as France) are less likely to be Eurosceptic;
- Protestants are typically the most Eurosceptic, and people living in traditionally Protestant and/or majority Protestant countries (such as the UK) are more likely to be Eurosceptic;
- Orthodox Christians tend to sit between the two, but are closer to the Catholic pro-EU position;
- Religious behaviour and belief are almost universally associated with being less Eurosceptic, regardless of the national context or one's religious community.

While the characterisation of how religion affects Euroscepticism is fairly straight-forward, however, the theories describing the mechanisms through which this relationship is manifested – particularly the effect of religious belonging – are not. Here, we group the main theories accounting for the effect of religious identity into three categories based on their focus: (1) the historic relationship between religious and political institutions; (2) the effect of religion on political ideology; and (3) the effect of religion on national identity. These are not contradictory accounts of why identification with particular Christian communities affects Euroscepticism; rather they are complementary and collectively account not only for why some religious communities are more Eurosceptic than others but also (as we argue in Chapter 6) why the voting behaviour of Britain's Christian communities has evolved over the past 40 years. After detailing the theories for how religious belonging affects Euroscepticism, we turn to religious behaviour and belief, which relate primarily to the influence of religious teachings and tenets, the cues from religious elites, and social capital.

Religious belonging and Euroscepticism: the history of political and religious institutions

Boomgaarden and Freire (2009) describe the EU as an institution with a distinctly 'Catholic nature'. Not only does the principle of European integration – in which a supranational institution possesses authority that supersedes that of national governments in certain areas of political and social life – adhere to a political structure they have been a part of and supported for centuries in the Catholic Church, but also the notion that Catholics are a community that transcends national borders is central to their identity (Madeley 2007; Nelsen and Guth 2003, 2015; Nelsen et al. 2011; Davie 2019; Guerra 2016). Moreover, the social and political values promoted by the EU are consistent with those central to Catholicism and frequently promoted by the Vatican, including charity, peace and social democratic conceptions of social justice (Coupland 2004; Madeley 2007). The history of European integration is the development of a political institution that fits closely with Catholic conceptions of their community and their preferences for international cooperation and supranational government. It is little wonder that many of the political parties that have most passionately advocated European integration have traditionally been related to Catholic values and communities, such as Germany's Christian Democratic Union (Nelsen and Guth 2015).

Protestantism, on the other hand, is characterised by a break with the Catholic Church and/or a rejection of notions of transnational religious communities and supranational authorities. Historically, many Protestant communities have relied on strong national governments to protect them from the persecution and dominance of the Vatican and its allies (Nelsen and Guth 2015; Scherer 2020). They have an interest, therefore, in protecting the sovereignty of the nation-state and are unlikely to find the idea of pooled sovereignty and supranational institutional authority appealing.

Indeed, the Euroscepticism of many Protestant communities originated in their view of European integration as a means of achieving Catholic dominance through a 'pro-integrationist nexus of the Catholic hierarchy and Catholic politicians' at the core of the European project (Philpott and Shah 2006: 63). In addition, many Protestant denominations – such as the Church of England – have played and continue to play a key role in the shaping of national identities. European integration may be perceived as a threat to the clarity of such identities, not only because it weakens national borders and pools political power but also because of the stated objective of the EU to facilitate the growth of a European identity (McLeod 1999; Scherer 2020). Some such communities have even played a direct role in national government, policy-making, policy delivery and legislating, meaning that any loss or pooling of sovereignty at the European level poses an even more direct challenge to their social and political standing and influence (Smith and Woodhead 2018). The Church of England was key, for example, to delivering welfare and social policy in England and Wales for centuries, its senior bishops are still appointed by the Prime Minister, and both its budget and rules are subject to parliamentary oversight (McLean and Linsley 2004). For an institution so closely connected to English national identity and government, it is easy to see how Anglicans could perceive anything that weakens or challenges the English national identity and the British state to be a threat or challenge to their own church.

In short, it is easy to see how the history of Catholicism and Protestantism, and the way this was interwoven with the formation of modern Europe and countless European wars, would predispose certain religious communities towards a more or less supportive view of European integration. Anybody identifying with such communities, or raised in families identifying with such communities, would be exposed to lived experiences, beliefs and values that could shape how they view the effect of European integration on the identity, status and even security of their religious community. The result, numerous studies have argued, is a less Eurosceptic outlook among Catholics and a more Eurosceptic outlook among Protestants (Nelsen et al. 2001, 2011; Nelsen and Guth 2015; Scherer 2020; Guerra 2016; Smith and Woodhead 2018). That said, while history would lead us to expect Catholics to be more supportive of European integration, and Protestants to be more wary of it, we should not ignore the recent path of integration that has given many Christian leaders cause for concern (we return to this below).

While political history gives a good insight into how Catholicism and national church Protestantism might affect Euroscepticism, it is a less informative guide of how free church Protestants might view the process. The existing literature does not distinguish between Protestant communities when studying religion and Euroscepticism; however, we argue that this is extremely problematic because not only do different Protestant communities express differing support for European integration (Kolpinskaya and Fox 2019), but also their distinct history means they cannot be expected to view the process in the same way. Free church Protestants share the rejection of Catholic notions of transnational community and supranationalism of national church Protestants, but they do not play the same role in the articulation of a national identity or national government, and they do not have the same relationship with the state that may predispose them to be wary of its power waning. Indeed, many free church Protestants were persecuted by the state for failing to recognise the authority of the national church; Methodists and Baptists in Britain, for example, were labelled 'non-conformists' and persecuted by the government and the Church of England. While such communities may have less reason than Catholics to welcome European integration, therefore, they also have less reason than national church Protestants to fear it. (Kolpinskaya and Fox 2019; see also Chapters 3 and 4).

Religious belonging and Euroscepticism: political ideology

> maintaining a religious affiliation is traditional and socially conservative given a wider environment of public and private secularity. . . . [signifying] deference to the past, to long-established institutions and to the values of older generations.
>
> (McAndrew 2017b: 6)

Identification with a religious community also implies a range of social and political values that are informed by the beliefs of that community and its theology. In some cases, there is a direct link between a theological belief (such as the belief in the God-given Ten Commandments identifying stealing and killing as sins) and a political ideological belief (such as the view that thieves should be prosecuted and abortion should be illegal). In others, the link may be less direct and reflect the historic values and practices of Christian communities, such as the exclusion of women from public life based on the belief that they were created subordinate to men and were more culpable for original sin (Ruether 1998). Subscribing to such beliefs or even being exposed to them may inform socially conservative (and patriarchal) views about society, the family, the workplace and the social interactions within them. In addition, simply identifying with long-established institutions and values indicates a deference to traditional institutions, beliefs, practices and sources of authority, as well as a reluctance to see such deference rejected or weakened at a social level, that would predispose people towards socially conservative views (McAndrew 2017b).

Whatever the source of these religiously inspired social and political values, they can become key elements of an individual's political ideology, that is, the principles, ideas and values that guide political decisions and action (Clarke et al. 2017). They help shape the way people view the social and political world and inform their beliefs about how the world should be and what policies should be pursued to deliver it. The socially conservative values and dispositions promoted by religious communities, therefore, and reinforced by one's identification with religious communities and institutions, ultimately encourage a tendency towards social conservatism in the political ideology of Christian voters (Clements 2015; Flanagan and Lee 2003). As a result, such voters tend to believe in respect for the authority and the role of traditional social institutions (such as the church or family) and support policies that promote or protect them. They are more likely to feel that conforming to the moral standards and beliefs derived from such institutions is more important than individual autonomy or freedom of expression, and that serious deviation from such values could even be socially damaging. The most high-profile expression of this tendency is in opposition to same-sex marriage (or sometimes homosexuality outright) and abortion, but they are also apparent in religious communities tending to be more supportive of capital punishment and tougher punishments for criminals in general (Clements 2015). Social conservatives also tend to be communitarian, believing that one's identity and social obligations are based more on their connections to their local community and the people within it than to people, beliefs or issues elsewhere (Smith and Woodhead 2018; Ford and Goodwin 2017). Such a belief is particularly apparent among Protestants, whose churches are often rooted in localised communities and promote such communitarian values (Smith and Woodhead 2018). Change to communities, such as that brought about through European integration or mass migration, is seen as at best undesirable and at worst damaging to community identity and cohesion (Krouwel and Kutiyshi 2018; Ford and Goodwin 2017; Hobolt 2016; Richards et al. 2019).

Socially conservative voters are the bedrock of Euroscepticism throughout Member States because of the numerous ways in which European integration challenges their beliefs and values. First, EU membership brings with it the potential for mass migration (particularly in more economically developed nations in Western Europe), and with it the challenges to cultural, linguistic, ethnic and behavioural cohesion many social conservatives see as key markers of their communal and/or national identity. Second, European integration implies the pooling of national sovereignty within European institutions. Even if the outcome is beneficial, this arrangement is unlikely to please social conservatives who view the weakening power, influence and status of their national, long-standing governing institutions with disdain. They are also likely to view European elites and citizens as members of different communities, with distinct beliefs, values and priorities, and therefore doubt their capacity and/or willingness to act in the best interests of people from other communities.

Finally, and particularly important for the religious origin of some socially conservative values, the increasingly secular nature of the EU is at odds with their preference for deference to long-established religious institutions and beliefs (McAndrew 2017b). For national church Protestants, the right and capacity of their religious institutions to enforce their religious and social beliefs is often seen as a distinctive element of their society that should be preserved. The role of the Church of Scotland, for example, in shaping the moral values and practices that help define 'Scottishness' and Scottish national identity, is seen as a vital and distinctive feature of their society by Scottish social conservatives, and the desire to ensure that the established church can continue its role as the moral and spiritual guide of the nation is as much a part of religious voters' social conservatism as their other social and political values (Steven 2010; Heath et al. 1999; Kiss and Park 2014). Not only does European integration threaten this by weakening (or pooling) the sovereignty of the national government, but also the increasingly secular trajectory of European integration suggests a potential for European institutions to challenge or reject the values prioritised by those voters in the future.

From the early 2000s, for example, Catholic and Protestant churches alike expressed increasingly strong reservations about the direction of European integration, its social policy and the perceived democratic deficit of European institutions (Mudrov 2015; Minkenberg 2009; Flood and Soborski 2018). The flagship non-discrimination policies of the EU, for instance, are frequently at odds with the Catholic Church's views on women's ordination into the priesthood, reproductive rights, equal rights to marry for homosexual couples, and so on (Minkenberg 2009). As one Catholic priest lamented:

> First Brussels will remove our independence, then they will give us mandatory abortion and euthanasia and homosexual "unions". These things are already part of law, don't you see, in certain countries of Europe. And that is all seen as enlightened and touted as Europe's commitment to "equality and justice".
>
> (cited in Mudrov 2015: 525)

Religious leaders have also repeatedly lamented the increasingly secular and technocratic nature of European institutions, seeing the more recent course of integration as at best a missed opportunity to build 'a civil, cultural, socially coherent and spiritually mature society' (Mudrov 2015: 515), and at worst a path to a 'post-Christian Europe' (Casanova 2006: 65; Minkenberg 2009). Although European leaders attempted to address this by formally including churches in the formal consultation framework of the European institutions and developing the EU's 'spiritual dimension' in the Lisbon Treaty (Hill 2009: 171; Leustean 2012; Clements 2015), such recognition was extended not only to Christian churches but to all confessional and non-confessional philosophical organisations of Europe, ultimately equating Christian churches with non-Christian faiths and secular communities (Mudrov 2015). This was particularly irksome to those who felt that the EU was (or should be) quite openly a Christian organisation, defined by its basis in Christian principles, and with a European citizenry that resembled a traditionally 'Christian' ethnic community (i.e. white) (DeHanas and Shterin 2018). The potential inclusion of Muslim countries such as Turkey, for example, was particularly problematic for Christians who held this view and a campaigning issue for political parties seeking to 'instrumentalise' Christianity as a source of exclusive national identity. This, Roger Brubacker (cited in Ryan 2019: 74) argued, challenged Christians' conceptions of their identity in so far as it was connected to Europe: '[w]e are Christians precisely because *they* are Muslims. Otherwise, we are not Christian in any substantive sense'.

Religious belonging and Euroscepticism: religion and national identity

National identity is routinely identified as one of the most important determinants of Euroscepticism (Boomgaarden and Freire 2009; Hobolt et al. 2011; McLaren 2007; Henderson et al. 2017; Ford and Goodwin 2014, 2017; Clarke et al. 2017). It is a challenging concept, partly because what it means to be, for example, 'English' or 'Scottish' or 'Welsh' is constantly evolving in both individual and communal mindsets (not least as political elites try to define them and shape political campaigns around them), and partly because people hold multiple national identities simultaneously (Brubacker and Cooper 2000; Kenny et al. 2019; Henderson et al. 2017). It can also have a range of effects on political attitudes and behaviour, which can vary even among those who hold the same nominal identity (Henderson et al. 2017). From the perspective of Euroscepticism, what matters is the way national identity is connected to conceptions of political expression, and how 'open' or 'exclusive' people who hold such an identity view it.

English national identity, for example, is largely 'exclusive', as it is firmly rooted in ethnicity, ancestry, language and religious identification (McCrone 2002; Kiss and Park 2014; Ford and Goodwin 2017). People who hold such an identity are likely to view those of different ethnic, ancestral, linguistic or religious backgrounds as 'not English' (regardless of how that other person identifies). 'British' national identity, on the other hand, is more 'inclusive', encompassing both ethnic and civic elements with greater emphasis on the latter (Heath et al. 1999; Tilley et al. 2004). It is related to conceptions of shared citizenship, respect for British government and rules, and support for its customs (Kiss and Park 2014). While this can lead to people holding a 'British' identity being intolerant of those who do not share such characteristics (and considering them 'not British'), their view of others is more contingent on their behaviour than their ethnic or ancestral characteristics. This makes Britishness a 'pan-national state identity' (McCrone 2002: 303) and more compatible with feelings of Europeanness (Kenny et al. 2019), whereas holding English (or to a lesser extent, Welsh) national identities was associated with a rejection of any notion of transnational identity – particularly beyond the borders of the UK (Henderson et al. 2017; Evans and Menon 2017).

Since the early 2000s, English national identity has become 'a cluster point for other attitudes and concerns . . . [including] hostility to European integration, the sense of absence of political voice, concern about immigration and support for parties of the right' (Henderson et al. 2017: 643). In other words, English national identity has increasingly become associated with socially conservative values, hostility to immigration, Euroscepticism and support for right-wing parties and ideologies. Unsurprisingly, voters who identified as 'English' and 'English not British' were by far the most likely to vote for Brexit in the 2016 referendum (Curtice 2017): Henderson et al. (2017) concluded that Brexit was 'made in England'. That said, those expressing 'Welsh' and 'Welsh not British' national identities were also more likely to be Eurosceptic and to support Brexit (Henderson et al. 2017; Fox and Pearce 2018). In Britain, only Scottish national identity was associated with support for EU membership and closer in characterisation to the more 'inclusive' British national identity.

European integration can evoke hostility from people holding exclusive national identities for several reasons. Those who feel their national identity is connected to or represented in a political institution whose power is constrained by integration (such as Parliament) could interpret EU membership as not only an unacceptable challenge to the power and identity of that institution but as a danger to their national identity and culture (Henderson et al. 2017). They may even feel that certain forms of government or political interaction – such as supranational government – are inconsistent with what it means to be a member of their national community (Peitz et al. 2018; Clarke et al. 2017). In addition, some may feel that the distinctive history and cultural features of their nation is threatened by the subsuming of them within the histories and cultures of other Member States within the EU, or are simply incompatible with being an EU member and adopting a European identity (Kenny et al. 2019). Finally, traditional conceptions of national identity are institutions frequently cherished by social conservatives; indeed, such identities sit at the heart of their communitarianism, and the social institutions they are attached to may be seen as a key component of that national identity. Any perceived challenge to national identity from European integration, therefore, could evoke the ideological opposition to it from socially conservative citizens described earlier.

The significance of religion in this regard stems from the links between some religious communities and national identity – particularly national Protestant churches, such as the Church of England or Church of Scotland. Their very existence was often defined by a rejection of supranationalism and the desire to establish a church that specifically represented and catered for a particular national community (Scherer 2020; Nelsen and Guth 2015). They were subsequently bound within the constitutional development of the nation-state, and other institutions closely related to English and Scottish national identities such as Parliament, the Commonwealth and the Monarchy (Gifford 2015; Heath et al. 1999). To identify with the national community such churches are attached to is frequently to identify with those churches themselves, even if one otherwise has few religious characteristics (McLean and Linsley 2004; Kiss and Park 2014; Heath et al. 1999; Smith and Woodhead 2018). Anglicans, for example, are frequently more likely than non-Anglicans to identify as English, while Presbyterians are more likely to identify as Scottish (Clements 2015; Smith and Woodhead 2018). The members and clergy of the Church of England and Church of Scotland often feel it is their responsibility to help shape their respective national identities and provide spiritual and moral leadership to their national flock 'seeking to influence public policy' and 'to further the highest interests of the people', respectively (Steven 2010: 69 and 92). Identification with national church Protestantism, therefore, is expected to facilitate the development of national identities that (in the case of Englishness) are associated with hostility to European integration and the consequences of EU membership. Moreover, members of such communities are disproportionately likely to reject the notion of transnational identities – such as European – that may be seen as rivals to their own national identity.

Religious communities that lack the same relationship with national identity are not as likely to hold to exclusive national identities. They are also less likely to object (or at least feel quite so passionately opposed) to alternative identities that transcend national borders, such as European. For this reason, free church Protestants are not expected to be as Eurosceptic as national church Protestants. Catholics, on the other hand, are expected to be more comfortable with the notion of a transnational identity; indeed, this is a feature of the Catholic community already, and one which implies a supranational moral leadership (Nelsen and Guth 2015; Madeley 2003). Not only are Catholics less likely to hold exclusive national identities that promote Euroscepticism, therefore, but they are expected to be more likely to embrace transnational identities that depress it (Nelsen and Guth 2015).

Religious belonging and Euroscepticism: party identification

The final means through which religious belonging affects Euroscepticism is its effect on our relationships with political parties. Party identification has a powerful effect on our political attitudes and behaviour. People who identify with a party are likely to feel invested in its success; this makes them more likely to vote for the party and support it in other ways (such as through making donations), and they may even join the party to campaign for it. Identifiers also take more of an interest in the fortunes of the party and are more receptive to political messages or campaigns 'their' party may promote. Party identification also shapes the way we receive political information more broadly: we are more likely, for example, to view the performance in office of a party we identify with positively and to discount information suggesting otherwise, and to view the performance or policies of a rival party negatively (van der Eijk et al. 2007). Finally, party identification also helps people interpret political information and events: if we encounter a new or complex political issue, for example, we are likely to look to 'our' party for guidance on how to respond to or interpret it, and what judgements to reach about it (Dalton 2013). On the question of whether EU membership is good for our country, for example, we are more likely to view EU membership favourably if 'our' political party – the party we trust to represent us and act in our best interests – says that EU membership is a good thing and campaigns for continued membership.

As we noted in Chapter 1, identification with a religious community has long been associated with a greater tendency to vote for and identify with certain political parties (Bochel and Denver 1970; Tilley 2015; Steven 2010; McAndrew 2017a), whereby political and religious battles, debates and relationships formed more than a century ago 'continue to resonate in the contemporary world' (Tilley 2015: 911; Wald 1983). This primarily reflects the historic association between those communities and political parties, rather than a clear ideological overlap (Tilley 2015). Just as Anglicans have a predisposition towards Euroscepticism because of the history between the Church of England, the British state and the Catholic Church, for example, they also have a predisposition towards voting Conservative because the Conservative Party historically promoted the status and influence of the Church of England in British government and society, and it opposed those parties (such as the Liberals) that challenged the established church. The historic relationships between Britain's Christian communities and its political parties are promoted through institutional memory, and the intergenerational transmission of partisan values within families. The stance of political parties on the question of Europe, therefore, has the potential to shape how religious communities that are historically close to those parties view the issue. Religious communities with a historic predisposition to identify with pro-EU parties – such as Catholics or free church Protestants, who have tended to identify with the Liberal/Liberal Democrats and Labour – can be expected to be less Eurosceptic. Those with a predisposition to identify with Eurosceptic parties – such as Anglicans and Presbyterians who have tended to identify with the Conservatives – can be expected to be more Eurosceptic because of the campaigning and messaging of their party.

Religious behaviour and Euroscepticism: elite cues and social capital

A universal finding in research on religion and Euroscepticism is that religious behaviour increases support for European integration (McAndrew 2020; Smith and Woodhead 2018; Boomgaarden and Freire 2009; Davie 2019; Mudrov 2015; Gifford and Wellings 2018). This has been shown for Catholics and Protestants alike and appears to have no relation whatsoever to religious belonging: regardless of the religious community in question, religiously active people are less likely to be Eurosceptic. The literature identifies two theories to explain this effect. The first is that it is the result of elite cues, in which the almost universally pro-EU sentiments of religious elites are expressed to their congregations and so affect their attitudes towards Europe. As we noted in Chapter 1, even though there are clear differences in the Euroscepticism of Christian congregations in Britain, during the EU referendum leaders of every major religion in the country stated their support for continued EU membership. Smith and Woodhead (2018) point out that the clergy of the Church of England is more evangelical in religious values than most of their flock: they espouse social and political values promoting global issues and tolerance for migration that stand in stark contrast with the communitarian values of most Anglicans. Similarly, the leaders of the Catholic Church have long identified European integration as beneficial for Europe and a means of advancing a Catholic social agenda (Boomgaarden and Freire 2009; Nelsen and Guth 2015). The result is that more active members of religious congregations are more likely to be exposed to religious values that promote support for European integration – or at least depress hostility towards some of the consequences of EU membership (such as immigration) – through their greater interaction with religious elites.

The second theory focuses on the consequences of religious activity for social capital. Social capital refers to the resource individuals can obtain from social networks that can be used to achieve communal or individual objectives (Fox et al. forthcoming). People who are more religiously active are more likely to have more developed and extensive social networks, and to come into more contact with people within their communities, meaning they are likely to have greater access to social capital (McAndrew 2020). Social capital has been associated with a host of beneficial outcomes for communities, such as lower crime rates, better health and education and more political participation (Putnam 2000). One such benefit is greater tolerance and social cohesion: social interactions promote the formation of friendships and bonds with others in one's community, as well as habits and values that facilitate cooperation and make people less suspicious of or intimidated by those from different cultural or ethnic backgrounds. Religious activity is just one way in which people can become more active in their communities, but it produces the same outcome of raising social capital and so raising tolerance for others and developing a belief in cooperation and communal obligations (Caputo 2009; Fox et al. forthcoming). McAndrew (2020) argues that this explains why higher levels of religious activity depress Euroscepticism: because the social capital that people develop makes them less likely to be hostile to European migrants, and more likely to develop values that are manifested by European integration and supranationalism, such as cooperation and transnational community obligations.

Religious belief and Euroscepticism: Christian tenets

Similar to religious behaviour, most literature that looks at how religious beliefs are associated with Euroscepticism conclude that those who hold stronger beliefs are less likely to be hostile to European integration, although the effect of religious belief is usually shown to be markedly weaker than that of belonging or behaviour (Boomgaarden and Freire 2009; Smith and Woodhead 2018; Nelsen and Guth 2015). This is because of the values that are promoted by the tenets of Christian faiths, such as charity, peace, mutual respect and tolerance. These not only encourage support for the principles behind European integration, but also discourage some of the attitudes frequently at the heart of Euroscepticism, such as intolerance of migrants or a rejection that one's obligations extend beyond one's own kin. People who hold stronger religious beliefs are more likely to hold and express these values in their daily lives and political attitudes, and so they are even more likely to exhibit the consequences of those beliefs, that is, more support for European integration, or at least less hostility towards it. As with religious behaviour, there is no suggestion that the effect of religious belief varies in any meaningful way between religious communities, not least because the differences between Christian communities are usually very limited when it comes to theology and religious tenets. Whatever the nuance of differences in belief between, for example, Catholics and Anglicans, they preach largely the same values and so their beliefs are expected to have similar consequences for Euroscepticism.

Conclusion

In this chapter, we have detailed the theoretical framework that underpins this research. We have outlined what is meant by 'religion', and what challenges there are in measuring the concept at the individual level. Drawing on the extensive literatures on religion and politics, Euroscepticism, and religion and Euroscepticism, we have also set out the dominant theories explaining why those religious characteristics are expected to affect how people feel about European integration. Over the following four chapters, we both test and elaborate on these theories in our examination of how religion is and has been related to Euroscepticism in Britain. In some cases, we find yet further support for established thinking of the relationship between religion and Euroscepticism, such as the tendency of religious behaviour to be associated with more support for integration. In others, we are able to offer more nuance to existing understandings, such as in showing that it is not Protestants in general that are more Eurosceptic but rather national church Protestants; free church Protestants lack many of the motivations towards Euroscepticism exhibited by their national church counterparts. Finally, in still other cases, our analyses challenge the existing theories and force us to re-evaluate the relationship between religion and Euroscepticism, such as our finding that Catholics are not, in fact, pro-EU but are actually characterised by greater Euroscepticism than the non-religious and free church Protestants. We consider the theoretical implications of our key findings for the future study of religion and Euroscepticism, including existing theories accounting for the relationship between the two, in our final chapter.

3 Euroscepticism and religion before Brexit

> British membership of a Community which . . . counts among its aims the reconciliation of European enmities, the responsible stewardship of European resources and the enrichment of Europe's contribution to the rest of mankind, is to be welcomed as an opportunity for Christians.
>
> Church of England General Synod on Europe in 1972 cited in Mudrov (2015: 515)

As with its departure 47 years after it joined, the UK's entry to the EC was legitimised through a national referendum in 1975 – the first nationwide referendum in the UK history. While many of the arguments deployed in that campaign were similar to those in 2016, the results were very different: 67 per cent supported EC membership. While not a ringing endorsement of European integration, it reflected the belief of most voters that closer integration with Europe was compatible with the UK's economic, cultural and political interests (Gifford and Wellings 2018). As European integration continued apace, however, and EU citizens gained the right to move freely throughout Member States, as British voters became less loyal towards and more critical of their political parties, and as those parties increasingly took for granted or ignored socially conservative Eurosceptics, British hostility to European integration became more widespread.

This shift towards an increasingly Eurosceptic outlook is clear among Britain's religious communities. In terms of religious communities' support for EC/EU membership, the 1975 and 2016 referendums are almost mirror images. As shown in Chapter 4, in 2016, the staunchest supporters of EU membership were the religiously unaffiliated, while the most passionate advocates of Brexit were Anglicans, with free church Protestants not far behind. A clear majority of Catholics and Presbyterians, meanwhile, supported Remain. In 1975, however, the religiously unaffiliated were the most opposed to EC membership, while Britain's Christian communities (particularly Protestants) were more supportive. As the quote given earlier illustrates, the Church of England (which did not take an official stance in the 2016 referendum) expressed clear support for the principle and objectives of European integration just prior to the UK joining the EC. While the entire British electorate was to become more Eurosceptic after 1975, the Anglican community stands out for a particularly pronounced change from being among the strongest supporters of European integration to among its fiercest critics – despite the stance of the Church of England's leadership barely changing.

In this chapter, we use the BES series of surveys to examine the effects of religion on Euroscepticism, first through its relationship with support for EC membership in the 1975 referendum, and then through its effect on attitudinal support for that membership over the following 40 years. We show how Britain's Christian communities evolved from endorsing EC membership in 1975 to adopting increasingly varied views by the 2000s, in which some (such as Catholics and Presbyterians) were more supportive of European integration while others (such as Anglicans) were among its fiercest critics, as the consequences of EU membership increasingly interacted with religious voters' distinct political and social ideologies and national identities. We also show that religious behaviour and belief have, in contrast with that of belonging, remained stable sources of sympathy for EC/EU membership, regardless of denominational membership. While their effects were consistently small, the perceptions that EU membership and mass migration were placing increasing strain on the homogeneity of British society and culture, as well as its political sovereignty and identity, were to some extent mitigated by the communal bonding effects and elite cues arising from greater engagement with religious institutions and values.

Religion and the 1975 referendum

Norton (2011: 53) called the issue of EC membership 'one of the most politically contentious issues in British politics in the last half of the 20th century': it split both the Conservative and Labour parties and cut through traditional left-/right-wing ideological allegiances. Vocal campaigners for and against EC membership could be found in both parties: Conservative Eurosceptics (such as Enoch Powell) did not wish to undermine the identity of Britain as a distinct island nation and world power, while Labour Eurosceptics (such as Tony Benn) feared the potential limitations EC membership could impose on a socialist government (Norton 2011). Eventually, the decision to join the EC was enshrined in the 1972 European Communities Act, but this did not prevent the issue from splitting both major parties for decades to come.

Labour Party leader Harold Wilson illustrated the difficult balancing act the party was trying to maintain, leading opposition to the specific terms of EC membership defined in the 1972 Act while remaining supportive of membership in principle, drawing support and criticism from all sides of the House of Commons and even from within his Shadow Cabinet. In an (ultimately successful) effort to hold his party together, Wilson charted the course that David Cameron was to follow 40 years later and committed to renegotiate the terms of EC membership and put the outcome to a referendum if Labour won the 1974 general election – a policy that was to persuade the former Conservative minister Enoch Powell to vote for the party (Norton 2011; Gifford and Wellings 2018). While it took two general elections that year to deliver a Labour majority, the commitment was eventually delivered and the referendum held – although (just as David Cameron was in 2016) Wilson was forced to suspend Cabinet collective responsibility and allow ministers to campaign freely to keep his government intact (Geddes 1999: 3).

The themes of the 1975 referendum campaign closely resembled those of the 2016 Brexit referendum. The key argument of prominent Conservative 'No' campaigners was that EC membership would undermine the UK's independence and status on the world stage, that it would be detrimental to parliamentary sovereignty and British democracy, and it would undermine the British national identity (Gifford and Wellings 2018). Left-wing Eurosceptics also focused on the impact of EC membership on parliamentary sovereignty, arguing that EC membership would 'erode the importance of the vote' and weaken the capacity for people without wealth to 'safeguard their futures' (BBC 1975). 'Yes' campaigners emphasised the opportunity for EC membership to arrest the decline of both the UK's economy and its global influence, and dismissed concerns about sovereignty as 'getting bogged down in a theoretical debate about paper sovereignty' (BBC 1975). While the electorate endorsed continued EC membership, they did not completely reject the concerns of the 'No' campaign; while polling showed that voters agreed EC membership would reduce the sovereignty of the UK, however, they were so disillusioned with the major parties and the Westminster politics that they did not perceive such a loss to be particularly lamentable (Gifford and Wellings 2018). The polls also showed that voters placed great value on what they perceived as Britain's special historic heritage, the culture and institutions (especially the Monarchy) that distinguished the UK from Europe, and its 'unique national identity' (Gifford and Wellings 2018: 271). They did not share the views of the 'No' campaign, however, that EC membership posed a threat to them.

If there is one reason, the results of the 1975 and 2016 referendums were so different despite the arguments for and against EC/EU membership being

36 Euroscepticism and religion before Brexit

so similar, it is because the calculation of how great a risk European integration posed to the distinctive culture, institutions, heritage and identity of Britain changed substantially in the intervening 41 years. This explains why the relationship between religious belonging and Euroscepticism changed so markedly in that period – and in some cases, even more dramatically than in the wider electorate. While voters who identified with religious communities in 1975 were more likely to be socially conservative and (in the case of national church Protestants) to hold exclusive national identities (such as English/Englishness) just as in 2016, they were less likely to view EC membership as a threat to those values during the first referendum. In addition, the extent of European integration, and power afforded to European institutions, was far more limited before the Maastricht, Amsterdam and Lisbon Treaties of the 1990–2000s. There was less reason, therefore, for historic concerns about the overlap between European integration and Catholic dominance that would later underpin Protestant hostility to EU membership to trigger a Eurosceptic response.

Christian voters in 1975 were not only characterised, however, by less reason to be Eurosceptic than in 2016 – they were less Eurosceptic than non-religious voters at the time as well, especially Anglicans. Figure 3.1 shows the support for 'Yes' and 'No' of the largest religious communities in the 1975 referendum (as well as the religiously unaffiliated). Hostility to EC membership was greatest – at 34 per cent, just over a point higher than the national result – amongst the non-religious, while it was lowest

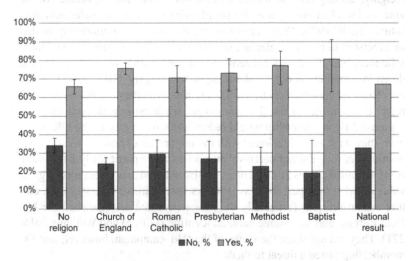

Figure 3.1 Vote in the 1975 referendum by religious denomination, per cent
Source: British Election Study 1975 Referendum Survey, post-election, face-to-face

amongst the Christian communities, and particularly Protestants. The most pro-EC were Baptists, only 19 per cent of whom opposed membership, and Methodists, of whom 23 per cent opposed it. They were closely followed by Anglicans, Presbyterians and Catholics, of whom 24, 27 and 30 per cent, respectively, voted 'No'. As we explain in Box 3.1, the difference between Anglicans and the non-religious is statistically significant, further supporting the view that at least some religious voters – and in this case, the largest Christian community in Britain – were more likely to support EC membership than the non-religious. While the data available to explain this pro-EU disposition among Anglicans are limited, it is likely to reflect the same values and identities that were to drive Anglicans towards a far more Eurosceptic position in later years. As described in Chapters 2 and 5, Anglicans are characterised by social conservatism and a strong sense of English national identity. While in 2016 these values led Anglicans to be more likely to perceive EU membership as a threat to the values, culture and institutions of their communities (local and national), in 1975 most voters felt that EC membership would protect and even promote the culture and prosperity of the UK. To the extent that Anglicans were more likely to prioritise British and English culture, institutions and identity, and to lament the strain placed on them by the decline of Britain's empire and global standing, they may well have perceived EC membership as a way of preserving and protecting those elements of British and English life they most cared about – a perception that was to change dramatically over the following decades.

Text Box 3.1 Tests of statistical significance

Throughout this book, we present confidence intervals that surround our estimates of the attitudes and/or behaviour of religious voters. These are 95 per cent confidence intervals and represent a measure of the uncertainty that surrounds our estimate of a particular trait in the population based on our identification of it in a survey sample. In the BES sample, for example, 76 per cent of Anglicans supported EC membership in 1975, and so we estimate that 76 per cent of Anglicans in the electorate did so too – but there is a degree of uncertainty around that estimate, which is represented by our confidence interval (i.e. the error bars) in Figure 3.1. When comparing differences between groups within the same sample, we can usually assume that instances where those error bars do not overlap indicate a statistically significant difference, that is, a difference present in the population as well. The error bars surrounding the estimate of Anglicans' support for 'Yes' in Figure 3.1 do not overlap with those for the non-religious, for example, and so we conclude that this is a meaningful, significant difference.

Frequently in our analysis, confidence intervals will overlap, and in some cases, even when the difference between two groups is as large as that between two other groups for which the confidence intervals do not overlap. In Figure 3.1, for example, 77 per cent of Methodists supported 'Yes' – even more than the 76 per cent of Anglicans – and yet the difference between Methodists and the non-religious is not statistically significant. This is because there are far fewer Methodists in the BES sample than there are Anglicans, meaning we have less data on which to base an estimate of support for EC membership in the wider electorate. This means we cannot be as confident in the specificity of our estimate, and the larger confidence intervals surrounding the Methodist estimate reflect this. This does not mean that there was no difference in the support for EC membership between Methodists and the non-religious, or that the estimate of 77 per cent of Methodists voting 'Yes' is worthless; it simply means that we cannot be confident the difference between Methodist and non-religious support for EC membership was replicated in the British electorate.

Where possible, we highlight differences that are statistically significant in our analyses, and we use a wide range of statistics and analyses to verify the importance of the data we present and the differences between voters exhibiting various religious characteristics. We also make the full tabular outputs for our regression analyses, as well as our data and coding files, available on the project website, so that readers can investigate the data and scrutinise the importance of statistical findings for themselves.

There were also clear 'religious effects' stemming from other religious characteristics. The 1975 BES does not include distinct measures of religious behaviour or belief but includes a measure of religiosity instead. This represents respondents' degree of religious commitment and the importance of religion in their lives, and is bound up with both their behaviour and their beliefs: in short, higher religiosity implies more religious behaviour and stronger religious beliefs (McAndrew and Voas 2011; Bruce 2018). Figure 3.2 shows that respondents who are more religious tended to be more supportive of EC membership, and these differences were statistically significant: more than eight in ten 'very religious' respondents voted 'Yes' compared with seven in ten who were 'not religious'.

Euroscepticism and religion before Brexit 39

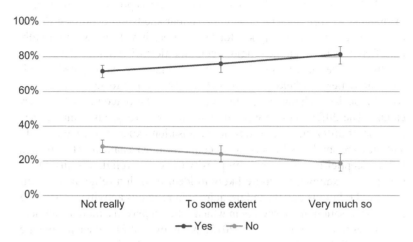

Figure 3.2 Vote choice in the 1975 referendum by religiosity, per cent
Source: British Election Study 1975 Referendum Survey, post-election, face-to-face

As we detailed in Chapter 2, this is likely to reflect religious voters' perception that values and objectives promoted by their faith are identifiable and achievable through European integration, such that the more strongly people held to those beliefs the more likely they were to support EC membership as a way of seeing them realised. It will also reflect the development of values emphasising tolerance, cooperation and the duty to help others even beyond one's national community, which are promoted through religious interaction, as well as the influence of cues provided by religious elites during religious activities (such as attending church). The Church of England, for example, endorsed the spirit and the aims of European integration during the General Synod on Europe in 1972, reflecting a propensity to support EC membership that would largely persist for the following 40 years (Mudrov 2015; Grebe and Worthen 2019; Smith and Woodhead 2018). The Vatican also consistently expressed positive sentiment regarding European integration from Pope Pius XII, who led the Church between 1939 and 1958 and 'gave all his support to the construction of the European community' (Mudrov 2015: 523), and which has remained the official position adopted by the Holy See ever since (Nelsen et al. 2001). The more religiously active someone was, the more likely they were to interact with religious elites and other members of the congregation who were also exposed to such cues, instilling and reinforcing a tendency to view EC membership as a way of promoting and achieving Christian objectives.

In 1975, therefore, the effect of religion on Euroscepticism was quite easy to characterise: religious belonging, behaviour and belief depressed Euroscepticism and promoted support for EC membership. There were virtually no differences between the religious communities: what mattered most was whether people identified with a religious community, participated in religious activities and held religious beliefs. This is not to say that religion was the decisive characteristic that determined the outcome of the referendum. The differences between how members of religious communities, or those of differing religiosities or socialisation experiences, were small, and they are smaller still once we account for other characteristics related to Euroscepticism and/or one's propensity to express religious traits. Older people, for example, are more likely to identify with a religious community, hold religious beliefs and participate in religious activities, reflecting their socialisation into a society in which religion played a more prominent and widespread role (Clements 2015; Wuthnow 2002). Older people are also more likely to be Eurosceptic as a result of having been socialised into a UK that was not part of the EC or EU and when the 'normal' state of affairs was not for the UK to pool sovereignty with other countries (Fox and Pearce 2018; Down and Wilson 2013). We need to account for the influence of these characteristics when identifying the effect of religion, therefore, to avoid biased estimates of how important and influential religion actually was.

To do this, we use regression analysis: a statistical technique that allows us to examine how a trait such as religious identification and religiosity is related to support for EC membership *while accounting for* the effect of other characteristics also related to EC membership, such as age or gender.[1] We modelled the likelihood of BES respondents voting 'No' in the referendum, depending on their religious denomination, religiosity and childhood religiosity, while controlling for age, education, gender, trade union membership, party identification and attitudes towards immigration.[2] The results of the model are reported in Figure 3.4. We used the results of the regression analyses to predict the average probability of someone who identified with a religious community voting 'No' in the referendum (i.e. expressing Euroscepticism) after the control variables were accounted for, and these probabilities are plotted in the graph.

The analysis shows that most of the differences in Euroscepticism between people with different religious characteristics were actually the result of other characteristics exhibited by those who were more likely to identify with a religion or have been raised in a religious household – such as being older. That said, there remained clear differences in the probability of Christians voting 'No' and the non-religious, comparable in magnitude to those shown in Figure 3.1. On average, the religiously unaffiliated had a

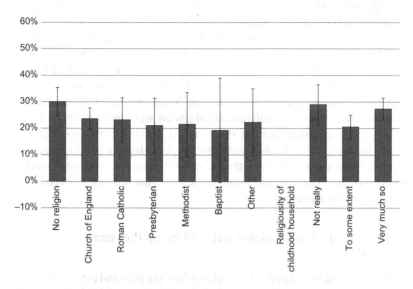

Figure 3.3 Predicted probability of voting 'No' in the 1975 referendum by religious belonging and religiosity of childhood home, per cent

Source: British Election Study 1975 Referendum Survey, post-election, face-to-face. Predicted probabilities calculated using STATA 'margins' command

30 per cent likelihood of voting 'No', compared with 24 per cent for Anglicans, 23 per cent for Catholics, and between 19 and 22 per cent for Presbyterians, Baptists and Methodists. In other words, while there was virtually no difference in Euroscepticism between Christian communities, there was a difference between Christians collectively and the non-religious. While only the difference between Anglicans and the non-religious was significant – and only at the 90 per cent confidence level – the small number of respondents in other Christian communities inevitably means that the confidence intervals are very large, and there is no evidence of a substantial difference at all between Anglicans and the other Christian communities. The data support the impression given by Figure 3.1, therefore, that differences between Christians in 1975 were negligible, but on the whole Christians were more likely to support EC membership than the non-religious.

Overall, these analyses show religion did play a role in shaping Euroscepticism in 1975. In general, Christians were more likely to support EC membership than the non-religious (significant at the 90 per cent confidence level), as were those who were raised in a somewhat religious household compared to a non-religious one (significant at the 95 per cent confidence level). The characteristics were exhibited by a large proportion of the British electorate; just over half of BES respondents were raised in a religious household, while only a third were religiously unaffiliated, and four out of ten were Anglican. The influence of their religious characteristics was nonetheless relatively weak – certainly compared with age (younger people were more likely to vote 'Yes'), education (those with more education were more likely to vote 'Yes'), attitudes towards immigration (those who were tolerant of migration were more likely to vote 'Yes') and party identification (Conservatives and Liberals were more likely to vote 'Yes').[3] To the extent that religion played a part in ensuring the UK remained a member of the EC in 1975, it had a positive but small effect on support for the institution – albeit one that was experienced by a majority of the electorate.

Religion and Euroscepticism after 1975: on the road to Brexit

In the years that followed the 1975 referendum, the pace and extent of European integration increased, and the impact of Europe – its institutions, priorities and people – on British political, social and economic life, national identity, culture and sovereignty grew. The result was not only an increase in Euroscepticism among those most likely to lament changes to some of the institutions, communities and identities most affected or challenged by Euroscepticism, but also an increase in the salience of the issue to British voters and politicians in general. Battles over Europe frequently dominated the political agenda throughout the 1980–1990s. Having supported integration in the 1970s, Margaret Thatcher's Conservative Party became increasingly divided over how to respond to it, with Thatcher herself passionately opposing the political integration proposed by the Maastricht Treaty eventually signed by John Major (Seldon 1998; Evans and Menon 2017). The Maastricht Treaty is identified as pivotal in the development of British Euroscepticism by Gifford and Wellings (2018) and Evans and Menon (2017), as many who supported economic integration in the 1970s balked at the move towards political and monetary integration now being pursued, and began campaigning for another referendum on membership in which they intended to lead the UK out of the institution.

After the bitter factional battles that consumed the Labour Party in the 1980s – leading to the breakaway of the Social Democrats in 1981 – Neil Kinnock's leadership brought an end to the dominance of left-wing Euroscepticism at the top of the party (Menon and Fowler 2016). Labour steadily shifted towards a less Eurosceptic position, even considering joining the single currency when it entered government in 1997. The New Labour government was able to effectively manage the issue of EU membership by largely keeping it off the political agenda (although the potential to join the Euro did lead to impassioned campaigns against the government and became a centrepiece of the 2001 Conservative election campaign) and focusing on domestic policy successes. This was not without difficulties, however, as it meant all but refusing to talk about Europe – giving free reign to Eurosceptic media and campaigners to fill the void and inflame hostility towards the EU (Menon and Fowler 2016). The government found they were unable to avoid discussing EU membership when the EU proposed overriding and consolidating existing EU Treaties into a single European Constitution, which galvanised the Eurosceptic movement (Blair 2011). Even though the proposal was rejected in French and Dutch referendums, the central propositions that had caused so much concern remained salient and were largely incorporated into the Lisbon Treaty. All the while, the free movement of people within Europe ensured that immigration became the most visible consequence of EU membership for most British citizens, with those who were sceptical about the benefits increasingly dismissed or ignored by Labour and (under Cameron) the Conservatives (McLaren 2003, 2007; Ford and Goodwin 2017; Evans and Menon 2017).

While many voters may have felt that EC membership did not threaten to change, weaken or dilute the values, communities and institutions they held dear in 1975, the direction and extent of European integration throughout the 1980s, 1990s and 2000s gave them reason to revise that opinion. They became increasingly sceptical that the benefits of EU membership were ever going to be realised by them and their communities, and (with some justification) that their concerns were taken seriously by their government or political parties. This not only increased their hostility towards the EU, and the salience of that hostility in shaping their political behaviour, but it also made them more receptive to the Eurosceptic, anti-establishment campaigns of insurgent political parties such as UKIP. UKIP highlighted the link between immigration and EU membership – fostering Euroscepticism among those predisposed to be critical of migration – and also linked the consequences of EU membership with a host of economic and social problems experienced by older, working-class and socially conservative voters and/or poorer communities in former industrial heartlands, including those relating to healthcare, housing, transport, employment, wages and crime (Ford and Goodwin 2014, 2017; Evans and Menon 2017).

An increasingly integrated Europe led to differences of opinion between the Christian communities that had largely endorsed EC membership in 1975. As we detailed in Chapter 2, national church Protestants were likely to be particularly critical, thanks not only to their greater social conservatism and tendency to identify with more Eurosceptic parties (principally the Conservatives), but also because of their strong attachments to traditional national identities and the role of their church in defining that identity. For them, EU membership increasingly brought threats and changes to the communities and institutions that defined their social lives, as well as diluting national identity and the distinctive social function of their church. The EU's support for policies – such as stem cell research and equal rights for homosexual relationships – only reinforced their view that the institution would not prioritise or protect the conservative values held by their religious communities. While the social conservatism of Catholics and free church Protestants may have given them similar cause to fret about the impact of integration and immigration on their communities, the development of a transnational European identity and the evolution of the EU into an increasingly powerful supranational authority saw Europe move closer towards a political arrangement the Catholic Church had long seen as a route to peace and prosperity. While free church Protestants may have had more reason to be Eurosceptic as well after 1975 – albeit not to the same extent as national church Protestants – Catholics may have found reasons to be both more supportive and more critical of European integration.

The change in the relationship between religious belonging and Euroscepticism

Figure 3.4 shows the levels of Euroscepticism in the British electorate – and for each religious community – from the 1983 to the 1997 general elections, and from the 2001 to 2015 elections. The two time periods are treated differently because the way the BES measured Euroscepticism changed in 2001. Before 2001, respondents were asked whether they supported leaving the EC/EU, and Figure 3.5 shows the proportion who felt that the UK should leave. From 2001, however, the question asked how satisfied respondents were with EU membership (the data show the proportion who were 'dissatisfied' or 'very dissatisfied'). As being dissatisfied with the EU is a less extreme form of Euroscepticism than demanding departure from it, we would expect the post-2001 question to show a greater proportion of Eurosceptics in the British electorate – and this is exactly what happened. While it is certainly possible that the number of British voters who felt that the UK should leave the EU, or were dissatisfied with EU membership, rose between 1997 and 2001, we cannot isolate this change from measurement effects in the data. Therefore, we discuss our findings with this caveat in mind and with specific references to the 1983–1997 and 2001–2015 time periods.

Euroscepticism and religion before Brexit 45

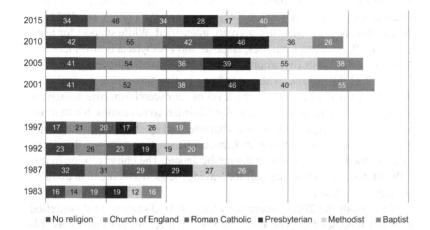

Figure 3.4 Eurosceptic attitudes in Britain by religious denomination, 1983–2015, per cent

Source: British Election Study, post-election, face-to-face surveys, 1983–2015 (weighted). The data reported as percentage of members in each group expressing Eurosceptic sentiment in each survey. The gap between 1997 and 2001 indicates the change in the methodology and the phrasing of the question measuring attitudes to European integration and the UK's EU membership

The bottom part of Figure 3.4 shows that while Euroscepticism rose between 1983 and 1987, it then fell again, and by 1997 slightly less than a fifth of voters felt that the UK should leave the EU. The data from 2001 suggest that plenty of those who supported EU membership may well have been dissatisfied with it, however, with close to half of voters dissatisfied with EU membership in 2001. This figure remained stable for the following ten years, and even fell slightly after 2010.

This stability masked variation within the electorate, however: as others have shown (and we discussed in Chapter 1), rising levels of migration from Eastern and Central Europe alongside the campaigning efforts of UKIP led to older, working-class and socially conservative voters becoming more Eurosceptic, while younger, socially liberal university graduates who had grown up with the UK as a part of the EU became less so (Ford and Goodwin 2014; Clarke et al. 2017; Hobolt and Rodon 2020; Fox and Pearce 2018). Such variation was also evident within the UK's religious communities. There were no significant differences in the desire to leave the EC between religious denominations and the religiously unaffiliated following the 1983 election. However, the percentage of those preferring to leave among all groups increased markedly in 1987, doubling to over 30 per cent of Anglicans and the religiously unaffiliated, and with almost as steep rises among Methodists as well. This greater Euroscepticism persisted among Anglicans (and the non-religious) throughout the 1990s as the debates about the Maastricht Treaty intensified. While support for leaving the EC/EU among Catholics, Baptists and Presbyterians also increased throughout the 1980s (by around 10 percentage points on average), by the 1990s it had fallen back, with around one in five supporting departure. In short, between 1979 and 1997, the level of Euroscepticism rose somewhat among the non-religious and the major Christian communities, but that rise was limited; rather, the period was characterised by short-term, and sometimes substantial, fluctuations in Euroscepticism that mirrored the dominance of the issue of Europe in the public debate. The one exception to this is the Methodists, whose support for leaving the EC/EU more than doubled between 1983 and 1997.

Throughout the 2000s, more than half of Anglicans were dissatisfied with EU membership. The only time this fell (to 46 per cent) was following the Conservative Party's victory after the 2015 election: given that during this period migration from the EU to the UK was reaching unprecedented levels, and the Eurozone was facing a debt crisis, multiple national bailouts and a refugee crisis (Curtice 2017), it is unlikely this represented an improvement in Anglicans' assessments of the benefits of EU membership for the UK. More likely is that this reflected an increase in their satisfaction regarding the issue of Europe in light of David Cameron's promise to renegotiate the UK's membership and hold an In/Out referendum, which the result of the 2015 election (in which, as we show in Chapter 6, Anglicans voted overwhelmingly for the Conservatives) ensured. Similar drops in Euroscepticism were apparent in other religious communities as well: by 2010, more than 40 per cent of Catholics were expressing disapproval of the UK's EU membership, but this figure fell by 6 points after the 2015 election. There were similar falls among free church Protestants, with Methodists displaying extraordinarily high levels of Euroscepticism in 2005 but becoming the least Eurosceptic Christian group by 2015. That said, Baptists bucked the trend somewhat, being the only group to become more Eurosceptic in 2015 (with 40 per cent being dissatisfied). It is unclear why Baptists would become more Eurosceptic at a time when the rest of the country was becoming less hostile to the EU and many Eurosceptic communities were evidently warming to the likelihood of a referendum on EU membership. The limited sample size of Baptists and Methodists in the BES, however, means that we should be cautious in over-interpreting short-term fluctuations that could easily be the result of statistical noise. Finally, Presbyterians showed a similar – but steeper – decline in Euroscepticism than Catholics and Anglicans, moving from 46 per cent disapproving of EU membership in

Euroscepticism and religion before Brexit   47

2001 to 28 per cent doing so in 2015. This may reflect the distinct political context of Scotland, in which the pro-EU Scottish National Party (SNP) had emerged the dominant political force in the country following the 2014 Scottish independence referendum, identifying EU membership as a source of security in the event they would be successful in breaking Scotland away from the Union. The only party promoting such a pro-EU stance in England at the time was the Liberal Democrats, whose popularity had reached unprecedented lows after their decision to go into coalition with the Conservatives in 2010.

Although religious attendance was not measured in all eight BES surveys, the association between more frequent attendance of religious services and support for UK's membership in the EC was evident throughout the 1983–1997, 2010 and 2015 data. Figure 3.5 shows how the effect of religiosity on Euroscepticism changed over that period. In every BES for which there are data available, religiosity was negatively associated with Euroscepticism, whereby those who never attend religious services were disproportionately more Eurosceptic than those who did so at all. While the effect was largely stable between 1983 and 1997, it became even more pronounced after the 2010 and 2015 elections: in the 1987 election, for example, the biggest difference was between those who never attended religious services and those who did so at all, with Euroscepticism 11 points higher among the former. Following the 2010 and 2015 elections, however, this difference rose to 15 and 21 points, respectively (all these differences were statistically significant at the 95 per cent confidence level).

We once again used regression analysis to isolate these religious effects from that of other characteristics related to Euroscepticism: age, gender, ethnicity, social class and education (a more limited range of controls were used to ensure comparability across the 1983 to 2015 BES).[4] We calculated the probability of being Eurosceptic (i.e. supporting leaving the EC/EU or expressing dissatisfaction with it) for members of each religious community, and those who participated in religious activities, in the 1983–1997 BES, the 2001–2015 BES and then the entire 1983–2015 series simultaneously. This allowed us to identify the average likelihood of, for example, an Anglican being Eurosceptic while controlling for their demographic and socio-economic characteristics *and* for the fluctuations in Euroscepticism that occurred from one election to another. Figure 3.6 shows the probability of each religious community, and those who did or did not attend religious services (regardless of their religious identification) being Eurosceptic in the 1983–1997 period, while Figure 3.7 shows the probability of each religious community being Eurosceptic in 2001–2015. As the data on religious attendance were not available in the 2001 or 2005 surveys, Figure 3.8 shows the data on religious identification and attendance for 2010 and 2015.

48 Euroscepticism and religion before Brexit

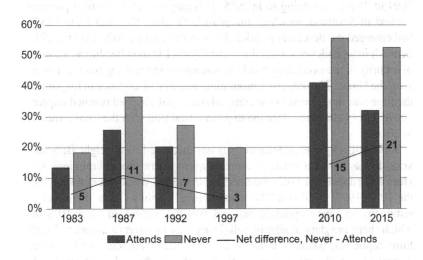

Figure 3.5 Leave/Disapprove of the UK's membership of the EEC/EU by religious attendance, 1983–1997 and 2010–2015, per cent

Source: British Election Study, post-election, face-to-face surveys, 1983–2015 (weighted). The data reported as percentage of members in each group expressing Eurosceptic sentiment in each survey. The gap between 1997 and 2001 indicates the change in the methodology and the phrasing of the question measuring attitudes to European integration and the UK's EU membership

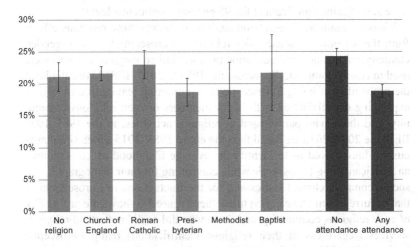

Figure 3.6 Probability of being Eurosceptic, 1983–1997, per cent

Source: British Election Study, post-election, face-to-face surveys, 1983–1997 (weighted). Predicted probabilities derived from logistic regression models. Predicted probabilities calculated using STATA 'margins' command.

Euroscepticism and religion before Brexit 49

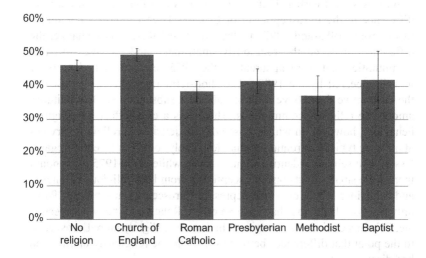

Figure 3.7 Probability of being Eurosceptic, 2001–2015, per cent

Source: British Election Study, post-election, face-to-face surveys, 2001–2015 (weighted). Predicted probabilities derived from logistic regression models. Predicted probabilities calculated using STATA 'margins' command.

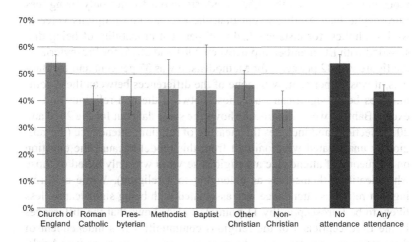

Figure 3.8 Probability of being Eurosceptic, 2010–2015, per cent

Source: British Election Study, post-election, face-to-face surveys, 2010 and 2015 (weighted). Predicted probabilities derived from logistic regression models. Predicted probabilities calculated using STATA 'margins' command. Details available in Supporting Information, available at: http://hdl.handle.net/10871/124138

As was shown earlier, Figure 3.6 confirms that there was virtually no difference in the Euroscepticism of Britain's largest religious communities between 1983 and 1997. To the extent that there was a change, the differences between the religiously unaffiliated and all five Christian communities that were apparent in the 1975 referendum had more or less disappeared by the 1980s. The short-term fluctuations identified in the descriptive data above did not indicate a substantial shift in attitudes among the religious communities. There was a clear effect for religious behaviour, however, in which those who participated in religious services at all were typically around 5 points less likely to be Eurosceptic, regardless of their religious identification. In short, while in the 1975 referendum there were small effects on Euroscepticism from both religious belonging and behaviour – both of which depressed Euroscepticism – by the 1980s, only religious behaviour had such an effect. Relative to the wider electorate, Britain's Christian communities had become slightly more Eurosceptic to the point that differences between them and the religiously unaffiliated had disappeared.

As with the descriptive statistics given earlier, the regression models also show that differences in Euroscepticism within the Christian communities started to grow after 2001. Anglicans emerged as the most Eurosceptic community, having on average a 50 per cent likelihood of being dissatisfied with EU membership, between 2001 and 2015. The other religious communities, on the other hand, stood out for not only being less Eurosceptic than Anglicans but than the average non-religious voter as well. Catholics, for instance, had a 39 per cent probability of being dissatisfied with EU membership between 2001 and 2015; for Presbyterians, the figure was 42 per cent; for Methodists, it was 37 per cent and for Baptists, it was 42 per cent, with none of the differences between these communities being significant, but those between the non-religious and all except Baptists were. Figure 3.8 shows the same data but for the 2010 and 2015 elections and includes the measure of religious attendance (the religiously unaffiliated were omitted from this model because the question on frequency of attendance at religious services was only asked of those who identified themselves as belonging to a religion). While confirming that religious attendance was associated with being significantly less likely to be Eurosceptic (by 11 points), it also shows that the differences in the Euroscepticism of the religious communities was independent of their respective tendencies to be more or less religiously active: Anglicans were by far the most Eurosceptic, having a 54 per cent probability of being Eurosceptic. The increase of this value from 50 per cent in Figure 3.7 reflects an increase in Euroscepticism among Anglicans after the 2001 and 2005 elections.

Catholics, Presbyterians, Methodists and Baptists were essentially indistinguishable, all having between a 41 and 44 per cent likelihood of being dissatisfied with EU membership.

One final point to note is that while on average there were clear differences in the Euroscepticism of religious communities (or, rather, of Anglicans compared with the rest) and those who were or were not religiously active, the effect of religion on Euroscepticism in any single election was small. As shown in other research (e.g. Fox and Pearce 2018 and the results in the online appendix), other characteristics controlled for in the regression analyses were more influential, particularly education and age.

Conclusion

This chapter has documented the evolution of the relationship between religion and Euroscepticism in Britain since the UK's first referendum on EC/EU membership in 1975. It shows a clear shift in the attitudes of Britain's Christians after 1975 as the nature of EC/EU membership – and what it meant for Britain's communities, institutions, and politics – changed. While they were broadly consensual in supporting EC membership in 1975, the religious communities became marginally more Eurosceptic throughout the 1980s, to the extent that the difference between them and the non-religious disappeared. The first signs of what was to become a large difference between Anglicans and other Christians also started to appear. Anglican Euroscepticism became far starker in the 2000s. As debates about the single currency and a European Constitution emerged, and as immigration from new Central and Eastern European Member States rose sharply, Anglicans became increasingly hostile to the effect European integration was having on their communities, British government and sovereignty, and English national identity. They emerged as by far the most Eurosceptic Christian community and exhibited even greater hostility to the EU than the non-religious electorate. As strains on public support for EU membership grew after 2010 – in light of the refugee and debt crises, and further increases in migration – Anglican Euroscepticism grew still further, to the extent that they were more likely than not to be dissatisfied with EU membership by the time David Cameron promised to renegotiate that membership in 2013.

It is, perhaps, remarkable that at the same time, Catholics, Presbyterians and free church Protestants became not only less Eurosceptic than Anglicans but non-religious voters as well. As noted earlier, for Presbyterians – who we would otherwise expect to be almost as Eurosceptic as Anglicans – this is likely to reflect them living in the most pro-EU country of the UK, with a more pro-EU media and governing party. For Catholics, we argue this partly reflects their support for the political objectives of European integration – and its obvious overlaps with the institutional organisation and objectives of the Catholic Church – which evidently trumped any concerns they may have had stemming from their social conservatism. The relatively pro-EU outlook of free church Protestants is harder to explain: while we would not expect them to be as Eurosceptic as Anglicans (lacking the same connection to English national identity and a church that is historically integrated with the British state and its sovereignty), we would expect their social conservatism to make them wary of the social changes brought about by integration and of some of the social policies promoted by EU institutions. It may suggest that Euroscepticism in the 2000s was driven far more by how attached religious communities were to English national identity than their inherent social conservatism, in which case the key difference between Catholics and free church Protestants on the one hand and Anglicans on the other is that the latter hold to strong, excusive conceptions of English national identity and the former do not. The limitations of the data available for this period make this, however, impossible to effectively test.

Finally, the focus in this chapter has been on how the attitudes of Britain's religious voters changed as the nature of the UK's EU membership evolved. We should not overlook, however, the role that religion played in helping to shape the attitudes of the British electorate as a whole, and its contribution to both the increasingly Eurosceptic nature of the electorate and the growing pressure on the Labour and Conservative parties to pay more attention to Eurosceptic voters. First, the increasing salience of Euroscepticism, national identity and social conservatism among the increasingly Eurosceptic element of the British electorate was in part driven by the effect that changes to the nature of the relationship between voters and parties and direction of European integration was having on religious voters. As Europe became more integrated and the consequences became more apparent and salient, the motivations that Christian communities had to be more or less hostile towards that process were 'triggered': the fact that almost half of the electorate identified with a religious community in the 2000s affected how likely they were to end up on one side of the Eurosceptic dimension that was becoming more important in shaping British public opinion.

Second, the secularisation of the electorate would also have both increased and decreased Euroscepticism and its salience for some. Fewer people identifying with Eurosceptically inclined religious communities would have meant fewer people having a reason (or as much of a reason) to develop Eurosceptic attitudes. At the same time, however, fewer people identifying with pro-EU communities, or participating in religious activities (Fox et al. forthcoming), would also have meant some voters were more receptive to Eurosceptic appeals than they may otherwise have been. The decline in the number of Anglicans has been far more pronounced than the decline in

Euroscepticism and religion before Brexit 53

the number of free church Protestants or Roman Catholics (Clements 2015; Bruce 2018), and so the net effect was likely to make the electorate overall less Eurosceptic than it may otherwise have been. Nonetheless, the increasingly Eurosceptic nature of Anglicans relative to non-Anglicans would have contributed to more than one in four British adults having more reason to be concerned by, or feel threatened by, European integration, and more receptive to the populist, Eurosceptic appeals of insurgent political parties. In short, while our focus is on how the political context and changes of this period affected the attitudes and behaviour of Britain's religious voters, we should not lose sight of the fact that the religious characteristics of the British electorate would also have contributed to the changes to the electorate described in Chapter 1 that ultimately heralded the most tumultuous period of modern British politics before, during and after the EU referendum.

Notes

1 We summarise the regression analyses and the results here. Readers interested in more detail of the regression models and full output tables can find more information in the Appendix.
2 These control variables were selected on the basis of important variables for explaining Euroscepticism identified in the academic literature: see Clarke et al. (2017), Fox and Pearce (2018), Curtice (2017), Ford and Goodwin (2017), McLaren (2003, 2007), Gabel (1998) and Hooghe and Marks (2005). It would have been preferable to have included other variables representing ethnicity and national identity, but such data unavailable in the BES.
3 The details of these effects can be found in the regression outputs in the Appendix.
4 The full details of the models and the outputs are available in the appendix.

4 Religion and the Brexit referendum

> God of truth, give us grace to debate the issues in this referendum with honesty and openness. Give generosity to those who seek to form opinion and discernment to those who vote, that our nation may prosper and that with all the peoples of Europe we may work for peace and the common good; for the sake of Jesus Christ our Lord. Amen.
>
> Church of England Referendum Prayer

The EU referendum campaign started officially on 15 April 2016. While the UK's political parties played a major role in it, as we have seen previously Euroscepticism is an issue that cuts across traditional party loyalties and left versus right ideological divides. The organisations leading the 'Remain' and 'Leave' campaigns, therefore, were run by and attracted voters, members and politicians from the Conservatives and Labour alike (the smaller parties were far more unified on the issue). Overall, the campaign was dominated by three issues: the economy, security and immigration (Startin 2018; Shipman 2017; Clarke et al. 2017). The official Remain campaign (Britain Stronger in Europe) focused on the negative consequences of leaving for the UK's economy and capacity to cooperate with other Member States on crime and terrorism. So relentless was the onslaught of messages from the political and economic elite of Europe and the United States (including President Barack Obama) that the Remain campaign had effectively 'won' the economic argument within weeks (Evans and Menon 2017; Clarke et al. 2017). It was far less effective, however, in dealing with the populist messages of the Leave campaigns (delivered by Vote Leave and Leave.EU) and their devastatingly effective demand to 'Take Back Control', which claimed that leaving the EU would restore powers to Westminster and enable the government to reduce immigration. Leave campaigners focused heavily on immigration, both its economic impact (such as pressure on wages and public services) and cultural impact (including on national identity) (Clarke et al. 2017; Startin 2018). While the Remain campaign tried to ignite fear of the consequences of leaving the EU, the Leave campaign appealed to the desires of socially conservative voters and those holding traditional, exclusive national identities to stop and even reverse the social, political and cultural changes that had undermined and challenged traditional communities and identities. McAndrew's (2020) analysis shows that the Leave campaign was particularly effective in activating the fears of cultural change and identity threat held by socially conservative voters with strong ties to English national identity.

Religion played almost no overt role in the campaign. To the extent that it was present at all, it was used in an indirect way to raise concern about migration. Religion is often invoked by right-wing Eurosceptics and populists as a justification for opposing European integration, who try to 'weaponise' Christianity and argue that the distinct identities and values of Christian communities are threatened by European integration – particularly plans in the 2000s for Turkish accession (Hobolt et al. 2011). A similar message was conveyed during the referendum campaign by Nigel Farage and Leave.EU, who raised a (greatly exaggerated) prospect of Turkish membership and the subsequent right of its residents to live and work in the UK. The infamous 'Breaking Point' poster – depicting a large queue of mostly non-white migrants and refugees and implying that they could be about to appear at the UK border above the words 'Breaking Point: the EU has failed us all' – was a not-so-subtle attempt to suggest that if the UK remained in the EU scores of migrants with different languages, skin colours and cultural and religious beliefs would soon come to the country.

Two campaigns were set up to try and win over British Christians, though neither featured in the national debate nor received any substantial media coverage (Wyatt 2016): Christians for Britain urged Christians to support Brexit, while Christians for the EU supported Remain. The founder of Christians for the EU – the Very Revd Michael Sadgrove – referred to the commandment to 'love they neighbour' and argued that walking away from an institution established to capture the ideals of partnership and collaboration would be wrong (Wyatt 2016). Adrian Hilton – author of the Archbishop Cranmer blog and co-founder of Christians for Britain – emphasised 'the need for the negation of evil through the dispersal of power' and argued that overly centralised government inevitably leads to corruption (Wyatt 2016). Although the Church of Scotland and Church of Wales both backed Remain, most of the major religious institutions in Britain – including the Church of England, the Catholic Church of England and Wales, the Muslim Council of Britain and the Board of Deputies (Carey 2016) – maintained a cautious, neutral line on the issue, although many religious figures openly expressed their opinions. On the one hand, this was a reasoned response to long-standing public scepticism about religious leaders exercising political influence while maintaining some level of political involvement, which is inevitable considering Church of England bishops sit in the House of Lords (Clements 2015; Steven 2010). Those religious leaders who did express a view, however, did so almost unanimously in opposition to Brexit. Most of the clergy of the Church of England, for example, openly supported continued membership (Smith and Woodhead 2018; Burgess 2016). The Archbishop of Canterbury – after previously not intending to take a public stance and suggesting that there was 'no correct Christian view, one way or the other' on Brexit (Burgess 2016) – outlined his case for EU membership in *The Mail on Sunday*, arguing that Christianity consisted of 'forward-looking' principles including sacrifice, generosity and vision beyond self-interest that were shared by the founders of the EU (Walters 2014). The Archbishop of York said that he 'hadn't heard a cogent argument' for Brexit, and that Britain should be 'reaching out' to friends and neighbours. From the Catholic Church, Cardinal Cormac Murphy-O'Connor, previously Primate of England and Wales, urged Catholics to vote Remain, and Archbishop Paul Gallagher, the Secretary for Relations with States for the Vatican, said he favoured a 'Remain' result (Corcoran 2016). Less than four weeks from polling day, 37 faith leaders wrote a letter in *The Observer* (2016) asking voters to '[t]hink of the wider world and vote to stay in Europe', including the former Archbishop of Canterbury Rowan Williams; Rabbi Laura Janner-Klausner of the Movement for Reform Judaism; Miqdad Versi, assistant secretary general of the Muslim Council of Britain; Bishop Thomas McMahon, retired Catholic prelate; Jasvir Singh, chair of the City Sikhs Network; the Rt Rev Dr Ian Bradley and Rev Dr Richard Frazer, both of the Church of Scotland; and Rabbi Danny Rich, Chief Executive of Liberal Judaism.

One of the few religious leaders to speak in favour of Brexit was the former Archbishop of Canterbury, Lord Carey of Clifton. Unlike his successors, he did not frame his argument in terms of explicitly Christian values or goals, but rather appealed to the need to reassert British sovereignty and democratic freedom: '[w]e should prize the ability to control our borders . . . The structures of the European Union are hardened against reform . . . For the British in particular, it is the loss of sovereignty and the inability of Britain or indeed any member state to reform and restore the democratic freedom of the nation state which have made the impositions of the EU such a running sore . . . If the prospect of being in control of our laws is not enough, we should prize the ability to control our borders' (Burgess

2016). While officially, most Christian organisations were neutral during the campaign, most of the religious elite eventually argued that Brexit was inconsistent with Christian values and political objectives and should be opposed. Just as it served to show how little attention British voters were paying to most of their political and economic elite, however, the referendum result was to highlight how out of touch particularly the clergy of the Church of England was with much of its congregation.

Religion and vote choice in the 2016 referendum

To examine how religion was related to support for Brexit during the referendum, we use the UK Household Longitudinal Study (UKHLS). UKHLS is particularly useful because it uses an exceptionally large sample of UK adults (around 40,000) and includes measures of all three dimensions of religion: belonging, behaviour and belief. The size of the sample allows more fine-grained analyses of not only how the three dimensions of religion affected support for Brexit, but how they interacted. Finally, UKHLS collects data on a range of political, economic and demographic characteristics, allowing us to control for many of the traits associated with religion and Euroscepticism that may bias our estimates of how religion was related to it in 2016.

UKHLS helpfully replicated the question put to UK citizens during the 2016 EU referendum: 'Should the United Kingdom remain a member of the European Union or leave the European Union?' (University of Essex, Institute for Social and Economic Research 2020). We identify as 'Eurosceptic' UKHLS respondents who supported Brexit. While this does not allow us to distinguish between those who did or did not vote in the referendum, it identifies support for Brexit regardless of political engagement. Following approaches taken in previous studies (see Clements 2015; Fox et al. forthcoming; McAndrew 2020), we measure religious belonging using respondents' self-identified affiliation with a religious denomination; religious behaviour by the frequency of their participation in religious services; and religious belief by how much of a difference they feel their religion makes to their daily life.[1]

Figure 4.1 shows UKHLS respondents' support for Brexit in 2016 based on their characteristics on the three religious dimensions.[2] Anglicans were by far the most likely to support leaving the EU – in fact they were the only group for whom a majority (55 per cent) did so. Methodists and Baptists were almost evenly split, with 49 and 46 per cent, respectively, supporting Brexit. The religiously unaffiliated were evenly divided but with a Remain preference – with 44 per cent supporting Brexit. Catholics and Presbyterians were the most pro-Remain Christian communities – with only 37 and 39 per cent, respectively, supporting Brexit. In short, the attitudes of Christian religious communities largely conformed to what we would expect based

58 Religion and the Brexit referendum

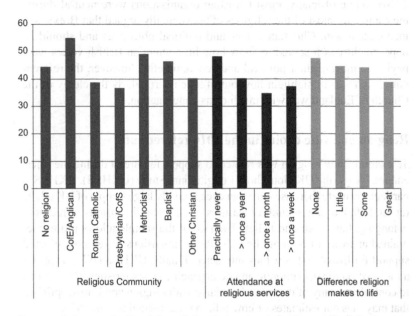

Figure 4.1 Support for Brexit by religious belonging, behaviour and belief, per cent

Source: UK Household Longitudinal Survey (UKHLS), Wave 8. Data weighted using UKHLS cross-sectional population weights and to account for sample clustering and stratification

on the theories detailed in Chapter 2. The exception are Presbyterians, who we would expect to have been similar to Anglicans in their Euroscepticism, but as we show below (and have discussed previously) this has more to do with Presbyterians living in the most pro-EU country in the UK than their religious values.

Figure 4.1 also shows once again the negative effect of religious behaviour on Euroscepticism. Almost half (48 per cent) of those who never attended religious services supported Brexit, compared with 40 per cent of those who attended at least once a year, and 36 per cent for those who attended at least once a month or weekly. In light of the overwhelmingly pro-EU stances taken by most religious leaders during the referendum campaign (see earlier), it is perhaps unsurprising that those who would have interacted with those religious leaders the most would have been most opposed to Brexit (Smith and Woodhead 2018). There was a similar – but weaker – effect for religious belief. Those for whom religion made no difference to their lives were the most likely to support Brexit, with 48 per cent doing so, compared with 45 per cent for those for whom religion made a little or some difference, and 39 per cent for those for whom it made a great difference. As

Religion and the Brexit referendum 59

we outlined in Chapter 2, this is likely to reflect the influence of religious values and tenets, promoting tolerance and inclusion, which would make religious believers less hostile to some of the consequences of EU membership perceived to be most negative by many social conservatives (such as immigration). The negative effects from religious behaviour and belief can also be explained through the social bonding effects of religion (i.e. its effect of enhancing social capital), which mitigates the perceived threat to one's communal and cultural identity (McAndrew 2020).

The large sample of UKHLS also allows us to examine how the three dimensions of religion interacted to affect support for Brexit. The data in Table 4.1 show that in addition to the differences between members of different religious communities, there were considerable differences within those communities depending on members' religious behaviour and/or beliefs. This reflects the independent effects that the three dimensions of religion have on Euroscepticism. Someone's religious identity may well encourage them to be more sceptical of the benefits of European integration, but their interaction with religious communities and strongly held religious beliefs could at the same time encourage a more supportive and tolerant view. This is particularly apparent for Anglicans: while 55 per cent supported Brexit overall, among those who never attended religious services, and who held few religious beliefs, the figure was 61 per cent. In other words, a lack of religious behaviour or belief reinforced the view of some Anglicans that EU membership was problematic. Among the most religiously active Anglicans, on the other hand, only 43 per cent supported Brexit, and among those with the strongest beliefs, only 46 per cent did so. For these Anglicans, their religious participation and beliefs offset the tendency towards Euroscepticism their religious belonging otherwise encouraged. When we consider how many Anglicans fit into these categories (see Table 1.1 in Chapter 1), we get a clearer idea of how important these religious effects were to the referendum result. Only a minority of Anglicans attended religious services monthly or weekly (19 per cent) and felt that religion made a great difference to their lives (16 per cent); only 10 per cent both attended religious services monthly or weekly *and* felt that religion made a great difference to their lives. Among these Anglicans, 57 per cent supported continued EU membership. Among the larger groups of Anglicans who never attended religious services (59 per cent), for whom religion made no difference in their lives (28 per cent), or who never attended services and felt that religion made no difference to their lives (23 per cent), support for Brexit was far greater: 61 per cent for those who never attended services or for whom religion made no difference and 64 per cent for those in both categories. In 2016, 23 per cent of British adults identified as Anglican; a fifth were Anglicans who practically never attended religious services or only did so once a year, and

Table 4.1 Effect of religious behaviour and belief on support for Brexit by Christian denomination, per cent

		No religion	Anglican	Catholic	Presbyterian	Methodist	Baptist	Other Christian
	Overall	44	55	39	37	49	46	40
Attendance	Practically never	45	61	47	43	62	53	47
	>Once a year	35	50	36	27	45	42	36
	>Once a month	40	41	31	22	29	42	35
	>Once a week	32	43	34	34	44	44	37
Difference religion makes	None	46	61	44	44	64	63	48
	Little	40	55	38	33	45	44	40
	Some	41	53	37	37	49	47	44
	Great	41	46	39	31	46	44	36

Source: UK Household Longitudinal Survey (UKHLS), Wave 8. Data weighted using UKHLS cross-sectional population weights and to account for sample clustering and stratification

Religion and the Brexit referendum 61

12 per cent felt that religion made little or no difference to their lives. To the extent that these religious characteristics made those voters more likely to support Brexit, we are looking at just over one in ten British adults whose self-identification as Anglican alongside their other religious characteristics made them more likely to support Brexit.

The pattern is similar (though less pronounced) for other groups. Almost half of religiously inactive Catholics supported Brexit, as did 43 per cent of inactive Presbyterians, compared with 34 per cent of the most active Catholics and Presbyterians. Meanwhile, 44 per cent of Catholics and Presbyterians for whom religion made no difference to daily life supported leaving the EU, compared with 39 and 31 per cent, respectively, among those for whom it made a great difference. While the effect of religious behaviour and belief was more or less the same as for Anglicans and Presbyterians, however, the importance of those characteristics for explaining Catholics' decisions in the referendum is greater because the proportion of Catholics who are religiously active, or for whom religion makes a great difference to their lives, is considerably higher. As shown in Table 1.1, for example, only 38 per cent of Catholics 'practically never' attended religious services in 2016, compared with 59 per cent of Anglicans and 57 per cent of Presbyterians, and 60 per cent of Catholics felt that their religion made 'some' or 'a great' difference to their lives, compared with 43 per cent of Anglicans and 45 per cent of Presbyterians.

For Methodists and Baptists, the pattern is similar to that of Catholics. Religious participation and belief made them more likely to support EU membership, and those characteristics had a greater influence on their communities' support for Brexit because a larger proportion of them were religiously active or held stronger religious beliefs. More than half (55 per cent) of Methodists attended church at least once a week, for example, as did 35 per cent of Baptists, and 57 per cent of Methodists, and 40 per cent of Baptists felt that religion made a great difference to their lives. Support for Brexit was similarly low among these voters, at around 44 per cent in each case, compared with just under two thirds of Methodists who never attended church, or for whom religion made no difference. Among Baptists, 53 per cent of those who never attended church, and 63 per cent of those for whom religion made no difference, supported Brexit. While identifying as Methodist or Baptist may have had the capacity to make people more Eurosceptic, therefore, most Methodists and Baptists are religiously active and hold stronger religious beliefs, leading most of them to oppose Brexit. That said, even though a majority of Methodists, Baptists and Catholics supported continued EU membership, these communities were far smaller than Anglicans, and so any impact on the result was more limited. Compared with 23 per cent of British adults who identified as Anglican in 2016, for example, 8 per cent identified as Catholic, 2 per cent as Methodist and 1 per cent Baptist. By far the most important 'religious effect' in the 2016 referendum (in terms of being likely to affect the result), therefore, came from identifying as Anglican.

Identifying the religious effects

As discussed in Chapter 3, identifying the effect of religion on Euroscepticism is challenging because of the overlap between religion, Euroscepticism and other characteristics related to both that can lead to unwarranted conclusions about the relationships between them. The extensive literature on characteristics related to support for Brexit, for example, shows that age was a key determinant of how people voted in the referendum, with young people far less likely to vote Leave than their elders (Fox and Pearce 2018; Clarke et al. 2017; Curtice 2017). Younger people are also less likely to identify with a religious community, participate in religious activity and hold strong religious beliefs (Clements 2015; Fox et al. forthcoming). The greater tendency of religious voters to support Brexit, therefore, may reflect their age as much as their religious characteristics. Similar confounding characteristics could include social class, education, ethnicity and even region (given the concentration of Presbyterians in Scotland and Anglicans in England, for example). While the data above clearly show considerable differences in support for Brexit between people of differing religious characteristics, therefore, how much of that difference is driven by religion cannot be determined from such descriptive statistics. As in Chapter 3, we use regression analysis to measure the effect of religious belonging, believing and behaviour on support for Brexit while controlling for socio-economic and demographic traits related to it:

- age, including age-squared and age-cubed to capture the curvilinear relationship between age and Euroscepticism;
- gender;
- education – with those with more education expected to be less Eurosceptic;
- occupational social class, housing tenure and current and prospective financial situation, reflecting economic status and resources expected to depress Euroscepticism;
- whether respondents' homes were in urban or rural communities, given that support for Brexit was higher in rural areas);
- region;
- and country of birth, so that foreign born nationals in the UKHLS sample who were more likely to support EU membership can be accounted for.[3]

Religion and the Brexit referendum 63

There are also ideological characteristics and national identities that are also related to both religion and Euroscepticism and that, if not controlled for, can lead to biased estimates of the effect of religion. Indeed, as we discussed in Chapter 2, such characteristics are argued to help explain why religious voters are more or less likely to be Eurosceptic and sit at the heart of most explanations for voters' support for Brexit and Euroscepticism in general (Hobolt 2016; Hobolt et al. 2011; Ford and Goodwin 2017; Clarke et al. 2017; Curtice 2017; Boomgaarden and Freire 2009; McAndrew 2020). Accounting for these in the regression analysis is more problematic, however, first because UKHLS does not include all of the measures necessary to do so. The second and more complex challenge, is that religion is not just correlated with these traits – we argue it is causally related to them as well. As we detailed in Chapter Two, our theory (and that of virtually every other study on religion and Euroscepticism) is that religion exerts an indirect effect on Euroscepticism through its impact on political ideology and national identity; that is, we do not argue that someone becomes more Eurosceptic just because they identify as Anglican, we argue that they become more socially conservative and more likely to hold an exclusive English national identity partially as a result of identifying as Anglican, and that this leads them to be more Eurosceptic. The regression techniques employed below and in Chapter 3 are suitable for estimating the effect of religion while accounting for the influence of characteristics that are correlated with it, or causally antecedent to it (such as age), but not for any effect that religion might have on other independent variables in the model. Trying to estimate the effect of religion while controlling for these other characteristics, therefore, not only violates assumptions underpinning regression analysis (that the effect of independent variables are independent of each other) but runs the risk of biased estimates of the effect of religion and those other controls (see McAndrew 2020).

We provide a way of partially overcoming this problem and identifying the complex indirect effects of religion on Euroscepticism in Chapter 5. Here, we limit our regression analysis to accounting for those demographic and socio-economic characteristics that are theorised to affect religion and/or Euroscepticism but are not affected by religion. This means our estimates of the effect of religion below cannot be interpreted as direct or indirect effects on support for Brexit (wrapped up within them will be, for example, the effect of religion on national identity, and of national identity on Euroscepticism), and they almost certainly over-estimate the effect of the dimensions of religion on support for Brexit. Our objectives are to (1) identify the effect of religion on Euroscepticism that is at least independent of causally prior demographic or socio-economic characteristics, (2) more robustly test the significance of the differences in support for Brexit between voters of differing religious characteristics identified earlier and (3) identify more robustly the contribution of religion to the UK's decision to leave the EU in 2016. None of these objectives are compromised by the challenges relating to ideological values and political identification outlined earlier.

Regression analysis results

The results of the regression analyses are summarised in the graphs below, expressed as the probability (as a percentage) of respondents supporting Brexit depending on their religious characteristics while accounting for the control variables.[4] Figure 4.2 shows the average probability of the religious communities supporting Brexit, and the error bars indicate the 95 per cent confidence intervals. In cases where they do not overlap, the difference between the two estimates is statistically significant. The fact that some of those confidence intervals are very large reflects the small number of people within that religious community within the UKHLS sample, and the inevitable result that we can have less confidence about how the average members of that community felt about Brexit.

As is clear in Figure 4.2, few of the differences between the religious communities that were identified in Figure 4.1 were significant. Anglicans, however, did stand out: with a 50 per cent likelihood of supporting Brexit even after the controls had been accounted for, they were by far the most Eurosceptic religious community. This was significantly higher than the religiously unaffiliated (who had a 44 per cent probability) and Catholics (45 per cent). Similarly supportive of Brexit were Baptists, with a 49 per

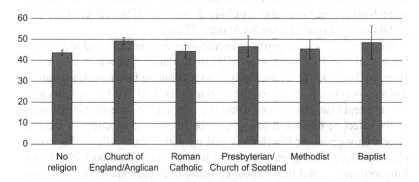

Figure 4.2 Probability of supporting Brexit, per cent

Source: UK Household Survey (UKHLS), Wave 8. Data weighted using UKHLS cross-sectional population weights and to account for sample clustering and stratification. Predicted probabilities calculated using STATA 'margins' command

cent likelihood, Methodists, with 46 per cent and Presbyterian, with 47 per cent – none of which were significantly different from Anglicans.

Figure 4.3 shows that there were also statistically significant differences depending on religious behaviour. Those who were more active were less likely to support Brexit: someone who 'practically never' attended religious services, for example, had a 47 per cent probability of supporting Brexit, compared with 40 per cent among those who attended weekly.

There was no significant difference between those who attended weekly, monthly or yearly – what mattered is that they attended at all. The effect of religious belief was similar but smaller: someone for whom religion made no difference to their daily life (i.e. held weaker beliefs) had a 46 per cent probability of supporting Brexit, compared with 44 per cent for those for whom it made 'a little difference'. There was no difference based on the extent to which religion made a difference, that is, holding religious beliefs to the extent that they had at least some effect on daily life was what mattered for depressing Euroscepticism.

The regression analyses also allow us to explain the mystery of why Presbyterians – whose characteristics should make them more likely to support Brexit than free church Protestants or Catholics – were among the most supportive of EU membership in the referendum. As we have noted elsewhere, the explanation is quite simple: more than four-fifths of

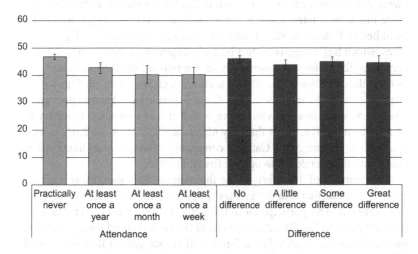

Figure 4.3 Probability of supporting Brexit attendance and difference, per cent

Source: UKHLS. Data weighted using UKHLS cross-sectional population weights and to account for sample clustering and stratification. Predicted probabilities calculated using STATA 'margins' command

Presbyterians live in Scotland, where average Euroscepticism is far lower than elsewhere in Britain, and in which there is a more pro-EU media and a governing party that views EU membership as a guarantor of Scottish security outside of the UK rather than a source of many of its problems. As a result, well over 60 per cent of Scots voted Remain in 2016, a stark contrast with the clear majorities who voted for Brexit in both England and Wales. Once we account for this fact in our regression model – by controlling for region – we find that Presbyterians were almost as Eurosceptic as Anglicans. Relative to their countrymen, therefore, Presbyterians were as sceptical about the impact of European integration on Scottish identity and institutions, and cultural homogeneity of their communities, as were Anglicans in England.

Figure 4.2 also reveals a finding for Catholics that goes against the expectations of the existing literature on Catholicism and Euroscepticism: despite their support for EU membership being notably higher than most (with only 39 per cent supporting Brexit), in the regression analysis we find that Catholics were as likely to support Brexit as other Christian communities and not nearly as distinct from Anglicans as Figure 4.1 suggested. Our analyses show that this reflects two factors. The first is that a sizeable minority of Britain's Catholics – around a fifth – were born outside the UK. UKHLS shows that around one in ten came from other EU Member States, and another one in ten from outside the EU. Those from other Member States had obvious reasons for wanting the UK to remain in the EU. The more important factor, however, was the high levels of religious activity exhibited by Catholics. Most Catholics regularly participate in religious services, which has a negative effect on Euroscepticism. Once this tendency is controlled for in the regression analysis, the remaining effect of identifying as Catholic is shown to have a far weaker, negative effect on Euroscepticism. We explore more about how Catholicism affects Euroscepticism in Chapter 5. What this analysis shows is that it was Catholics' tendency to be religiously active, rather than any ideological values or identities associated with being part of the Catholic community, that was most important in explaining their tendency to oppose Brexit in 2016.

A comparison of the effects of the three dimensions shows that it is religious behaviour that had the greatest impact on Euroscepticism. On average, someone who participated in religious services weekly, for example, had a 40 per cent likelihood of supporting Brexit compared with 47 per cent for those who never attended; a 7-point difference greater than the 5-point difference between identifying as Catholic and Anglican, or Anglican and those of no religion. Religious belief had by far the weakest effect, with those for whom religion made any difference to their lives being on average 2 or 3 points less likely to support Brexit.

Religion and the Brexit referendum   67

The regression analyses also confirmed the independence of the effects of the three religious dimensions, that is, regardless of one's religious community, the effect of religious belief and/or behaviour was constant and vice versa.[5] The descriptive statistics in Table 4.1 (as well as analyses in Chapter 3) suggested such independence and the potential for cumulative or even contradictory effects from the different dimensions of religion. The regression models confirmed this and showed that the difference in Euroscepticism between people who varied across several dimensions of religion could be substantial, far larger than those based on a single dimension. This is illustrated in Figures 4.4 and 4.5, which show the probability of members of the five religious communities supporting Brexit depending on their religious behaviour and belief, respectively. Figure 4.2, for example, showed that Anglicans were on average 5 points more likely to support Brexit than Catholics – but if we break this down by their respective religious behaviour, the gap widens. Anglicans who practically never participated in religious services had a 61 per cent probability of supporting Brexit, compared with 47 per cent for an inactive Catholic, and 34 per cent for Catholics who attended church weekly. In other words, the difference of 5 points based on religious belonging alone becomes 27 points when we add religious participation to the mix and compare the most and least Eurosceptic. Looking across Figures 4.4 and 4.5, we can see that the staunchest

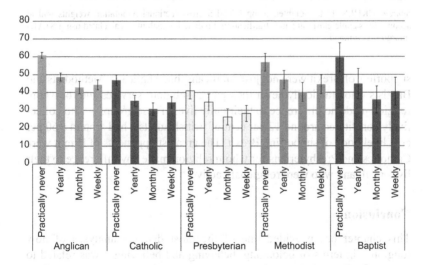

Figure 4.4 Probability of supporting Brexit by religious attendance, per cent

Source: UKHLS. Data weighted using UKHLS cross-sectional population weights and to account for sample clustering and stratification. Predicted probabilities calculated using STATA 'margins' command

68 Religion and the Brexit referendum

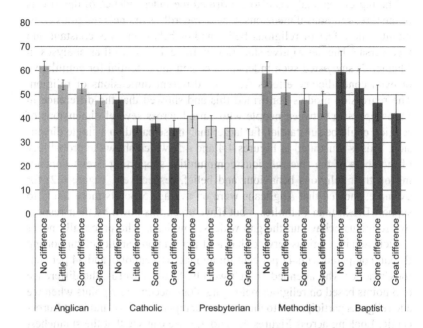

Figure 4.5 Probability of supporting Brexit by religious belief, per cent

Source: UKHLS. Data weighted using UKHLS cross-sectional population weights and to account for sample clustering and stratification. Predicted probabilities calculated using STATA 'margins' command

supporters of Brexit were not just Anglicans, but Anglicans, Methodists and Baptists who practically never took part in religious services and for whom religion made no difference to their daily lives. These groups – who collectively constituted around 12 per cent of British adults – had around a 60 per cent likelihood of supporting Brexit. The greatest opponents of Brexit were Catholics and Presbyterians for whom religion made any difference to their lives at all and who were religiously active.

Conclusion

This chapter has provided one of the most detailed analyses of how religion – in terms of belonging, behaving and believing – was related to support for Brexit in 2016 (for a similarly detailed analysis, see McAndrew 2020). As well as identifying which of Britain's religious communities were the most supportive of Brexit and the most opposed to it, this chapter has also shed considerable light on just how complex and substantial the effect of religion on Euroscepticism was during the referendum. This is the clearest demonstration in this book of how vital it is to take into account the effects of different manifestations of what it means to 'be religious' when examining how religion influences social attitudes and/or behaviour. Not only would a focus on a single manifestation (most commonly religious identification) mis-represent the effect of religion, but in the case of Euroscepticism at least it would almost certainly lead to an underestimation of the magnitude of that effect. As noted earlier, for example, the difference in likelihood of supporting Brexit in 2016 between those identifying as Anglican and Catholic was around 5 percentage points – a weak effect, dwarfed by that of other characteristics in the regression analyses such as education (someone with a degree, for example, was 26 points less likely to support Brexit than someone with no qualifications). The difference between a religiously inactive Anglican and a Catholic who went to church every week, however, was 27 points – comparable to the effects of traits frequently identified as the key determinants of voting behaviour in the referendum: age, social class and education. This is not to say that any research failing to account for religious belonging, behaviour *and* belief is invalid. Indeed, data limitations in many social surveys make future researchers being forced to focus on only one or two dimensions all but inevitable. Alongside the growing literature demonstrating the potential for different impacts from different manifestations of religion (e.g. McAndrew 2020; Clements 2015; Fox et al. forthcoming), this work highlights the need for clear theoretical justifications for omitting one or more dimensions and consideration of the potential implications for the empirical results.

Our analyses have shown that there were differences in support for Brexit between and within Britain's Christian communities in 2016, differences that started to appear as early as the 1980s (see Chapter 3) and had grown into – in some cases – wide gulfs that mirrored those between young and old or university graduate and manual worker frequently highlighted during the referendum campaign by the media. The staunchest supporters of Brexit among the Christian community were Anglicans, and particularly those who did not hold strong religious beliefs and were all but religiously inactive. These voters were likely to exhibit the social conservatism and strong English national identity that raised hostility towards the consequences of European integration, without any moderation stemming from the influence of Christian values, cues and encouragement from religious leaders or social capital based around religious social networks that would offset the perceived threat of integration to their communities. While Anglicans may have had numerous beliefs and identities that pushed them towards a pro-Brexit stance in 2016, however, religious activity had the potential to overcome these and push towards supporting Remain.

While few in numbers, religiously active Anglicans, or those with stronger beliefs, were more likely than not to oppose Brexit in 2016.

At the other end of the Eurosceptic spectrum were Catholics, who were the least likely to support Brexit. Contrary to the assumptions in much of the academic literature, this was not because the values or identities of Catholics predisposed them to support European integration (although it did make them less Eurosceptic than Anglicans), but because the majority were religiously active. This provided them with the social capital and religious cues that made them less likely to feel threatened or challenged by the consequences of integration (chiefly, migration) (McAndrew 2020). Similarly, supportive of EU membership were free church Protestants who held stronger religious beliefs or attended religious activities regularly – which describes most of those communities (see Table 1.1). The minority of religiously inactive Catholics, Methodists and Baptists, as well as those for whom their religion made no difference to their daily lives, were about as likely as the wider electorate to support Brexit in 2016. Finally, Presbyterians were located in-between Catholics and Anglicans. They were more supportive of EU membership than the latter, but only among the most religiously active, or those with the strongest beliefs, did that support rival that of Catholics. As noted earlier, however, it is important to remember the political context in which Presbyterians decided their views on the EU: in a staunchly pro-EU country. While Presbyterians were relatively pro-EU compared with Protestant communities primarily located in England and Wales, compared with the wider Scottish electorate they were unusually hostile towards the EU – this will be illustrated more fully in Chapter 5.

Finally, it is important to remember that when we talk about people exhibiting religious characteristics in Britain, we are talking about sizeable chunks of the population. As described in Chapter 1, only four in ten British adults exhibited no religious characteristics at all in 2016; almost half identified with a religion and a quarter identified with Christian communities (principally, Anglicans) that made them more Eurosceptic. While the proportion of adults exhibiting the combination of characteristics that prompted the most extreme support for or opposition to Brexit outlined earlier was small (just over a tenth of adults were religiously inactive Anglicans who did not hold strong religious beliefs, and around 5 per cent were religiously active Catholics with strong beliefs, for example), almost a fifth of British adults exhibited a religious characteristic that made them more likely than not to vote Leave on polling day, and more than a quarter exhibited characteristics that made them more likely than not to vote Remain. While there is little question that Britain is becoming a more secular country, and the effects of religion on political behaviour and attitudes are becoming limited to a smaller proportion of the electorate, this chapter has shown that the dismissal of religion as an important determinant of voters' behaviour and major political events in Britain is premature.

Notes

1 Respondents were invited to state whether they attended once a week or more, at least once a month, at least once a year, never or only for special occasions (such as weddings and funerals). Those who never attended or did so only for special occasions were merged into a 'Practically never' category. There is no direct measure of religious beliefs in UKHLS, but respondents are regularly asked what difference religion makes to their daily life – with answers including 'no difference', 'a little difference', 'some difference' and 'a great difference'. While not directly measuring religious belief, people for whom religion makes a great difference to their lives are more likely to hold beliefs that they feel are important than those for whom religion makes no difference. We assume, therefore, that those for whom religion makes a great difference to daily life are more likely to hold strong religious beliefs.
2 All our data is taken from Wave 8 of UKHLS collected between 2016 and 2018. While the panel design of UKHLS means that data on religion could have come from a prior wave, questions on respondents' religion are only included every four years, with a 'top-up' question used to collect data from those who did not take part when the question was asked of the full sample. Prior to Wave 8, therefore, most respondents' data were collected in Wave 4. While a common assumption in social research is that religion is a stable trait, it can be surprisingly volatile. Between Waves 1, 4 and 8 of UKHLS, for example, only 63 per cent of respondents who took part in all three waves reported the same religious identification, that is, between 2010 and 2018, around one in three UK adults changed their religious identity according to this survey. The reason for this is unclear; it could be that one in three adults genuinely did change their religious identification, or it could reflect measurement error, a change in how respondents consider their religious community or in the biases they have about answering the question, or all of the above. In any event, using data collected in Wave 8 of UKHLS is more likely to provide an accurate measure of UK adults' religious identification prior to the EU Referendum than data up to four years out of date.
3 See Fox and Pearce (2018), Clarke et al. (2017), Goodwin and Heath (2016), Fieldhouse et al. (2020), Hobolt (2016, 2018), Evans and Menon (2017), Halikiopoulou and Vlandas (2018), Ford and Goodwin (2017), Martin et al. (2019).
4 The probabilities were calculated from logistic regression models, which employed weighting, clustering and stratification variables provided by the UKHLS to account for uneven non-response and sample design. The full output of the regression models is provided in Online Appendix.
5 To test this, we added interaction effects between each religious identity and both religious behaviour and religious belief to the regression models. None were close to statistically significant.

5 Untangling (in)direct effects of religion on Euroscepticism

> The question of our political relationship with the other nations that comprise the present European Union is one which many of the Lord's people in Britain have always viewed with great apprehensiveness, given the political, social and religious influence of Romanism.
>
> Rev MacColl (2016)

In Chapter 2, we detailed the theories that explain why religion is expected to affect Euroscepticism, and which provide the basis for our interpretation of the data presented in Chapters 3 and 4. As we noted in Chapter 1, however, while these theories have been extensively debated and applied in previous research, the mechanisms they describe are rarely robustly tested (with the notable exceptions of Boomgaarden and Freire 2009; McAndrew 2020). This is an understandable limitation to the existing literature: the theories that account for the relationship between religion and Euroscepticism imply a complex network of causal effects that are difficult to represent in survey data or statistical models, and all but impossible to represent using the data and methods most commonly employed in this field (cross-sectional, multi-country surveys analysed using descriptive statistics and linear regression models). A robust test of those theories requires survey data including measures of not only religious characteristics and Euroscepticism but also the mediating characteristics that are expected to link them – including national identity, political ideology, party identification, elite cues and social capital – and statistical methods better suited to testing complex causal theories. It is nonetheless a problematic limitation: not only are we forced to rely on largely untested theories to explain important relationships but opportunities to add to those theories using insights gained from empirical analysis are missed.

In this chapter, we add to the small literature – consisting of Boomgaarden and Freire (2009) and McAndrew (2020) – that has overcome some of the challenges associated with testing the religion and Euroscepticism theories and provided valuable insights into how the two are related. We use the British Election Study Internet Panel (BESIP) data from before, during and after the Brexit referendum and structural equation modelling to examine how religious belonging and behaviour affect Euroscepticism *through* their impact on the identities and values at the heart of the theories detailed in Chapter 2: social conservatism, left/right ideology, party identification and national identity. We also include attitudes towards immigration, first because studies arguing that religion has no effect on Euroscepticism – including Boomgaarden and Freire (2009) – frequently point to such attitudes as the variable that accounts for the spurious relationship between the two, the omission of which leads to biased results. Second, because migration is, for many, the most visible consequence of EU membership, and hostility towards it frequently identified as the key determinant of Euroscepticism (e.g. Clarke et al. 2017; Ford and Goodwin 2017; McLaren 2003). Finally, because the effects of social conservatism and national identity on Euroscepticism are argued to stem from the increased intolerance of migration and its consequences they promote. Its inclusion, therefore, allows a more detailed study of the theorised causal chain between religious belonging and Euroscepticism. The use of attitudes towards immigration measures also allows us to overcome a limitation of the EU referendum BESIP data, which do not include measures of either social capital or exposure to religious elites, therefore, limiting our ability to test the theories for how religious behaviour is related to Euroscepticism. Greater tolerance for migration and its consequences, however, is argued to be the result of religious behaviour (and belief) that reduces Euroscepticism, and so we can at least look at how religious behaviour is related to Euroscepticism through its impact on tolerance for migration. There are, unfortunately, no measures of religious belief in BESIP – although as preceding chapters have shown, the effects of religious belief (when they are apparent at all) are far smaller than those of behaviour or belonging. Finally, we also take advantage of BESIP's rich measures of Euroscepticism to provide a more detailed analysis of how religion affects it, by looking at the effect of religious belonging and behaviour on voters' assessments of the costs and benefits of EU membership and their support for the principle of European integration itself. This allows us, in short, to identify whether religion makes voters more critical of the performance of European institutions and the consequences of membership for their country, or whether it makes them more hostile to the principle of European integration itself.

Structural equation modelling and the relationship between religion and Euroscepticism

The key empirical contribution of this chapter stems from two methodological innovations. First is the use of panel data – that is survey data collected from the same individuals repeatedly over a sustained period – allowing us to make causal claims with far greater confidence because we can directly observe how characteristics at point A (such as religious belonging) affect characteristics at point B (such as national identity) which in turn affect Euroscepticism at point C. This is in contrast with cross-sectional data, which measures information from a single point in time and with which the temporal ordering of characteristics must be assumed but cannot be observed. Second is the use of structural equation modelling: a statistical method well suited to testing complex causal theories because it can test the empirical validity of theoretical models based on their adherence to observed relationships within a dataset, and allows for a multitude of direct and indirect effects to be accounted for (Chin 1998; Carmichael and Brulle 2017; Kelloway 1995). This is a substantial advantage over regression analysis, which assumes (as we show in Figure 5.1) that all independent variables affect the dependent variable directly and simultaneously and cannot easily account for relationships *between* independent variables. In fact, it assumes that are none. Violating this assumption is frequently unproblematic (which is why regression analysis is so widely used in social research), but in cases

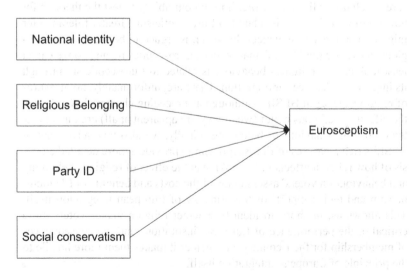

Figure 5.1 Conceptual map of Euroscepticism – regression analysis

Untangling (in)direct effects of religion on Euroscepticism 75

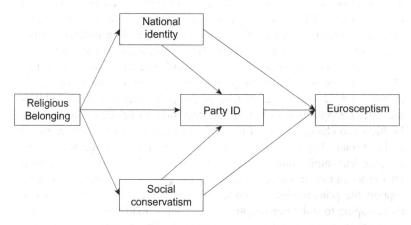

Figure 5.2 Conceptual map of Euroscepticism – structural equation model analysis

where there are expected to be multiple important relationships between independent variables it becomes a problem. As we illustrate in Figure 5.2, our theories for how religious belonging affects Euroscepticism expects multiple indirect relationships through the impact of religious belonging on national identity, party identification and social conservatism – not to mention the expectation that both national identity and social conservatism will affect one's likelihood of identifying with a political party that shares them.

A regression analysis is incapable of modelling such complexity and would mis-specify the relationships between the variables: non-significant and small effects may lead to the conclusion that those variables were unimportant, when in fact they have a considerable impact through other independent variables. SEM is capable of accounting for such complexity and estimating both the direct and indirect effects of independent variables on dependent variables.

The effect of religion on utilitarian and affective Euroscepticism

Throughout this book, we have defined Euroscepticism as a generalised hostility towards European integration and the EU, or some element of them, measured using single indicators representing support for leaving the EU or disapproval of EU membership. While straight-forward, this overlooks the considerable variation between different expressions of Euroscepticism or elements of integration against which it can be directed (Leruth et al. 2018). Some oppose EU membership, for example, because of the limitations it implies on state sovereignty, while others may have no problem

76 Untangling (in)direct effects of religion on Euroscepticism

with the principle of integration but are dissatisfied with the performance of EU institutions. While each may result in a similar attitudinal or behaviour outcome – hostility towards the EU – they are based on different values and perspectives and so are qualitatively different forms of Euroscepticism with different consequences. Euroscepticism based on the assessment that EU institutions are performing poorly, for example, can be more readily changed should institutional performance or policy change (Down and Wilson 2013). Opposition to European integration on principle, however, is far harder to change – even if the individual perceives EU membership to be beneficial, they may still oppose the institutional arrangement. There are practical implications as well: politicians hoping to improve support for European integration are more likely to have success among those who support the principle but are unhappy with institutional outcomes, while those hoping to stoke Euroscepticism will find a highly receptive audience among those opposing integration on principle. By accounting for different dimensions of Euroscepticism, therefore, we are able to get a far richer and detailed understanding of the way it is related to religion, and so enhance as well as test existing theories (Kolpinskaya and Fox 2019).

Efforts to better capture the complexity of Euroscepticism have led to the development of multiple conceptual models based around distinct dimensions of the attitude, that is, forms, modes or expressions that, while fundamentally representing hostility towards European integration, are based on different objections, values or perceptions of integration and its consequences (Lindberg and Scheingold 1970; Krowel and Abts 2007; Wessels 2007; Boomgaarden et al. 2011; Sørensen 2008; Vasilopoulou 2018). All of these different approaches recognise, however, a fundamental difference between Euroscepticism based on opposition to the principle of European integration and supranationalism – or 'affective' Euroscepticism (AES)– and that reflecting the failure of membership or EU institutions to achieve their objectives or deliver prosperity – or 'utilitarian' Euroscepticism (UES) (Lindberg and Scheingold 1970; Down and Wilson 2013, 2017).

In Chapter 2, we detailed the theories that explain how and why religion affects Euroscepticism. Here, we briefly revisit those expectations and elaborate on which dimension of Euroscepticism religion is expected to affect before we set out how we test them and then present our findings.

(1) *National identity*. National church Protestants (Anglicans and Presbyterians) have a historic connection to the institutions that have defined and governed their respective nations for centuries and play a key role in defining that national identity. This not only makes Anglicans and Presbyterians more likely to express their respective national identities but to reject identities – such as European – that may be to challenge or

dilute them, or that resemble historic claims to Catholic universalism. This should manifest as increased affective Euroscepticism (AES) amongst Anglicans and Presbyterians: they are more likely to object to European integration on principle because of its impact on their national identities and churches, regardless of the utilitarian consequences. Free church Protestants do not have the same history with national identities or nation states; they are defined by their historic rejection of the national church and were frequently persecuted for it. We would expect, therefore, Methodists or Baptists neither to oppose European integration on the grounds of its impact on national identity, nor to reject transnational identities, to the same extent as national church Protestants. Finally, a defining feature of Catholicism is that it is a transnational community led by a supranational authority; Catholics are not historically connected to specific national identities but to the notion of a transnational identity. They should be more supportive, therefore, of a European identity – depressing their AES – and less likely than national church Protestants to fear the impact of integration on English or Scottish identities.

(2) *Social conservatism.* Identification with any long-established religious community is a demonstration of inherent social conservatism, and participation in that community is expected to reinforce socially conservative beliefs about the importance of traditional institutions, community life and individual freedom. Members of any of the Christian communities are expected to be more socially conservative than the religiously unaffiliated, which should increase AES because of the impact of integration on the status and power of traditional social and political institutions, the impact of European migration on community change, and the socially liberal policies increasingly advocated by European institutions. This could also lead to increased utilitarian Euroscepticism, if such voters perceive that the impact of EU membership on their communities, country and identities is not just wrong in principle but produces harmful outcomes. All five denominations, therefore, should exhibit greater social conservatism and, therefore, stronger UES and AES.

(3) *Left/Right ideology.* Some religious communities are also characterised by more right-wing ideological views, particularly when it comes to welfare policy. Anglicans and Presbyterians have a history of supporting economically right-wing political agendas (primarily espoused by the Conservative Party), which support lower taxes and less welfare spending, while Catholics and free church Protestants have been more likely to support left-wing agendas promoted by the Liberals, Liberal Democrats and Labour Party. While Euroscepticism is prominent among voters with both left- and right-wing values, during the Brexit

referendum left-wing voters were more likely to vote 'Remain' (Fox and Pearce 2018; Clarke et al. 2017). Hence, Anglicans and Presbyterians are expected to be more Eurosceptic than Catholics, Baptists and Methodists in our analysis. We expect the consequences of left/right ideology to be realised primarily through UES, reflecting the different policy preferences the religious communities are likely to exhibit.

(4) *Party identification.* Finally, the social conservatism and left/right ideological characteristics of religious voters affects their tendency to identify with political parties, which in turn affects how likely they are to be receptive to the stances on EU membership of those parties. During the Brexit referendum, both major parties were severely divided but there was nonetheless a clear tendency for Conservative and UKIP identifiers to support Brexit while Labour, Liberal Democrat, Green and SNP identifiers were more likely to vote Remain (Fox and Pearce 2018; Clarke et al. 2017). Anglicans' and Presbyterians' propensity to identify with the Conservatives, therefore, should have made them more likely to support Brexit and share Conservative Eurosceptics' views about the negative consequences of EU membership (particularly, immigration), while the propensity of Catholics, Methodists and Baptists to identify with Labour and the Liberal Democrats should have made them less Eurosceptic. We have no clear expectation of party identification affecting one dimension of Euroscepticism more than the other.

(5) *Social capital and elite cues.* The negative effect of religious behaviour on Euroscepticism is expected to be realised through the consequences of social capital strengthening one's community bonds and their confidence in the identity of their community – and of elite cues promoting evangelical values of tolerance and global civic obligations. As noted earlier, we cannot measure this effect directly but we can measure the effect of religious behaviour on tolerance for migration, with the expectation that tolerance is higher for those (regardless of religious community) who are more religiously active. This should, in turn, lead to both weaker UES and AES, as negative assessments of the consequences of migration are based on its perceived impact on identifies, values and traditional institutions (i.e. affective concerns) and tangible economic and social (i.e. utilitarian) concerns.

Analysis details and results

Details of the SEMs

To test these theories, we constructed three SEMs – one each for England, Scotland and Wales – accounting for the different political and religious

Untangling (in)direct effects of religion on Euroscepticism 79

contexts of the three countries, as well as their distinct national identities. We used data from BESIP Wave 6 (W6), collected in May 2015 after the general election, Wave 7 (W7) collected in April/May 2016 before the EU referendum and Wave 8 (W8), collected in May/June 2016, during the referendum campaign. Data on religious belonging were taken from Wave 6, based on respondents' self-reported religious identification. We measured behaviour using respondents' attendance at church, categorising them into 'not religious', 'practically never', 'less than once a year', 'at least once a year', 'at least twice a year', 'at least monthly', 'at least fortnightly' and 'weekly or more'.[1] The sample was limited to respondents for whom there was complete data on all required variables: this left 7,022 respondents for England; 1,590 for Scotland and 962 for Wales.

Two measurement models were used to represent UES and AES, that is, models representing each based on data from numerous variables (the opportunity to use which being a further advantage of using SEM over regression analysis). The data were taken from Wave 8, each measured as a scale with higher scores implying greater Euroscepticism. UES was measured using respondents' views on five statements about the consequences of EU membership that capture their assessments of its worth (Kolpinskaya and Fox 2019). These were measured on 5-point Likert scales – from 'strongly disagree' to 'strongly agree' – recoded to be positively correlated: 'the EU has prevented war', 'the EU has made Britain more prosperous', 'the EU has brought people from different EU countries closer together', 'the EU has undermined the powers of the UK Parliament' and 'the EU has allowed too many members to join'. The AES scale consisted of responses to three questions. Two were 5-point Likert scales as above, capturing responses to the statements 'some laws are better made at the European level' and 'the British Parliament should be able to override all EU laws'. Rather than capturing respondents' assessments of what the EU has done or how EU membership has affected the UK, these capture their beliefs about the powers EU institutions should have relative to UK institutions, thereby reflecting their support for the principle of European integration. The third was a commonly used European integration scale, in which respondents are invited to express their support for integration on a scale from 0 (meaning their Member State should unite fully with the EU) to 10 (meaning the Member State should protect its independence) (Gabel 1998).[2]

The characteristics linking religious belonging and behaviour with Euroscepticism were measured using data from BESIP W7:

- Liberal/Conservative using a scale ranging from 0 (liberal) to 10 (conservative) produced by the BESIP team based on respondents' agreement with five statements about social values: 'Young people today don't have enough respect for traditional British values', 'For some crimes, the death penalty is the most appropriate sentence', 'Schools should teach children to obey authority', 'Censorship of films and magazines is necessary to uphold moral standards' and 'People who break the law should be given stiffer sentences';

- English/Scottish/Welsh/European national identity using scales running from 1 ('Not at all English/Scottish/Welsh/European') to 7 ('Very strongly English/Scottish/Welsh/European');
- Left/Right using a scale capturing respondents' left/right ideological beliefs, on which they place themselves from 0 ('Left-wing') to 10 ('Right-wing');
- Immigration – using respondents' views on whether immigration was good or bad for the economy, and whether it enriches or undermines cultural life (each on a scale from 1 to 7, which were merged into a single scale). Higher scores implied more positive views of immigration;
- Party identification based on whether respondents identified with the Conservatives, Labour, Liberal Democrats or UKIP – and in Scotland and Wales, the SNP and Plaid Cymru, respectively.

Figure 5.3 below illustrates how we expected religious belonging and behaviour to affect AES and/or UES through its impact on these mediator variables, and in some cases through causal relationships between the mediator variables, as outlined earlier. The rectangles indicate observed

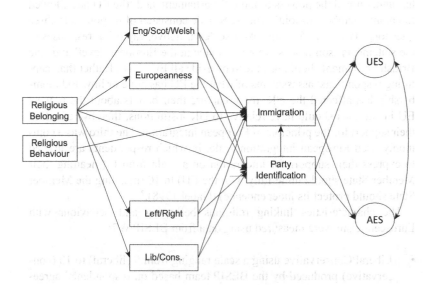

Figure 5.3 Hypothesised relationship between religion and Euroscepticism

Untangling (in)direct effects of religion on Euroscepticism 81

variables, while the circles represent the measurement models used to represent UES and AES. One-headed arrows indicate 'directional' (i.e. causal) effects – with a change in the variable at the beginning expected to produce a change in the variable on the end. The double-headed curved arrow between UES and AES represents a covariance.[3] Note that while the diagram includes a single variable for religious belonging and party identification, this is for presentational parsimony – the models included separate variables for Anglicans, Presbyterians, Catholics, Baptists and Methodists and for Conservative, Labour, Lib Dem, UKIP, SNP and Plaid Cymru.

SEM results

The results of our analyses for England, Scotland and Wales, respectively, are summarised in Figures 5.4–5.6. The diagrams focus only on the religion and Euroscepticism relationships – non-significant effects or significant effects not related to the link between religion and Euroscepticism are not shown to keep the graphs as straight-forward as possible. The full tabular outputs of the SEMs are available in Supporting Information. The figures next to the directional effects represent standardised coefficients ranging from 0 to 1; these are comparable within and between models. Effects below 0.1 are considered negligible; between 0.1 and 0.2 are weak; between 0.2 and 0.4 are moderate; and above 0.5 are strong (Chin 1998).[4]

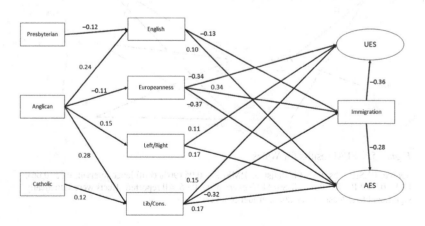

Figure 5.4 SEM results for England

Source: BESIP. Obs: 7,022. Fit statistics: RMSEA – 0.05 (90% confidence interval: 0.05–0.05). CFI – 0.96; SRMR – 0.03. UES – AES covariance = 0.92. All reported effects were statistically significant to at least 95 per cent confidence level

82 Untangling (in)direct effects of religion on Euroscepticism

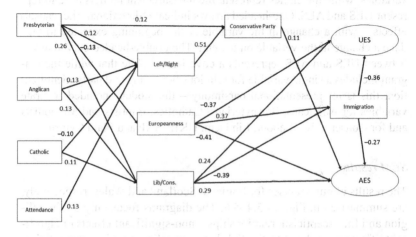

Figure 5.5 SEM results for Scotland

Source: BESIP. Obs: 1,590. Fit statistics: RMSEA – 0.05 (90% confidence interval: 0.05–0.06). CFI – 0.96; SRMR – 0.03. UES – AES covariance = 0.92. All reported effects were statistically significant to at least 95 per cent confidence level

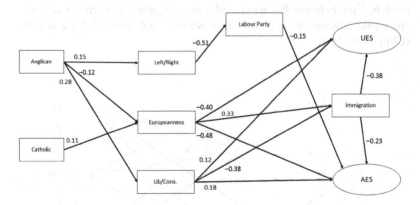

Figure 5.6 SEM results for Wales

Source: BESIP. Obs: 962. Fit statistics: RMSEA – 0.05 (90% confidence interval: 0.05–0.06). CFI – 0.96; SRMR – 0.03. UES – AES covariance = 0.96. All reported effects were statistically significant to at least 95 per cent confidence level

All three models confirmed most of the expectations regarding mediator variables outlined earlier. Holding an English national identity increased both AES and UES. It directly increased AES and indirectly increased both AES and UES because stronger English national identities were associated with decreased tolerance of migration. Holding a European national identity reduced both AES and UES, and this effect was similarly both direct and indirect through its impact on attitudes towards migration. Being more right-wing was associated with greater UES and AES, though in all three countries this effect was weak. Social conservatism had a much stronger effect, as it increased both UES and AES directly *and* had an indirect effect by reducing tolerance for migration. Attitudes towards immigration consistently had the strongest effects on both UES and AES – though the effect on UES was stronger. The one result that went against expectations was that for party identification, which had virtually no impact on Euroscepticism. The only exceptions were weak effects from identifying with the Conservatives in Scotland (which increased AES) and with Labour in Wales (which reduced it). For the most part, however, party cues had next to no impact on British Euroscepticism during the referendum: voters' social conservatism and national/European identities (or rejection thereof) were far more important.

The effects of these mediators were even more important because there were no direct relationships at all between religion (whether belonging or behaviour) and either dimension of Euroscepticism. The effects of religion stem entirely from its impact on political ideology, national identity and attitudes towards immigration, some of which were substantial. Anglicans throughout Britain were more likely to be socially conservative and economically right-wing, and to reject any notion of a European identity, while those in England were more likely to hold an English national identity. In Wales, Anglicans tendency to be right-wing made them less likely to identify with Labour (an effect not found in England or Scotland). The result was that Anglicans were by far the most Eurosceptic Christian community: their English national identities made them more likely to oppose the principle of European integration, while their rejection of European identity, social conservatism and tendency towards being right-wing further undermined their support for integration *and* led them to view the consequences of EU membership negatively. In addition, their social conservatism and national identities made them more hostile towards migration, which further increased both dimensions of Euroscepticism. While the individual effects stemming from Anglicanism were small, the *cumulative* effect of all the indirect relationships between Anglicanism and both dimensions of Euroscepticism were substantial, as shown in Table 5.1. By far the strongest religious effect on Euroscepticism in Britain stemmed from identifying as Anglican.

Presbyterians in Scotland were – in terms of Euroscepticism – virtually identical to their Anglican counterparts in England and Wales, as shown in Figure 5.5. They were more likely to be economically right-wing and socially conservative, less likely to identify as European and more likely to identify with the Conservative Party. All of this contributed to Presbyterians being more critical regarding the costs and benefits of EU membership and more hostile to the principle of integration (although the effect of being more right-wing in this regard was limited to the consequence of making them more likely to support the Conservatives). Their social conservatism and rejection of European identity also increased their hostility towards immigration, further increasing their Euroscepticism. One surprising finding in the Scottish model is that identifying as Scottish did not affect Euroscepticism: our analysis found that Presbyterians and (to a lesser extent) Catholics were more likely to identify as Scottish than those outside those communities, and Anglicans were less likely to do so, but this did not affect either UES or AES. While its connection to its Scottish national identity is an important feature of Presbyterianism, therefore, it was not something that affected the community's support for EU membership.

The effects of Catholicism in all three countries were generally weaker than those of Anglicanism or Presbyterianism, but the directions of those effects were similar, that is, identifying as Catholic increased Euroscepticism. This reinforces the argument advanced in Chapter 4: that while many Catholics support EU membership, identifying as Catholic does not promote that support – it is other characteristics related to being Catholic (namely religious participation) that accounts for their stance. In both England and Scotland, the analyses showed that Catholics were more likely to be socially conservative. This increased their opposition to the principle of European integration and their hostility towards immigration, which further undermined their support for integration and led them to reach more negative conclusions about the costs and benefits of EU membership. Catholics in England and Scotland were also no more likely to identify as European. This is against theoretical expectations and also helps explain the higher than expected degree of Euroscepticism among the Catholic community: without such an identity they lack an expected source of sympathy for European integration. Catholics in Wales, however, stood out for being no more socially conservative than non-Catholics and for being more likely to hold a European identity, as shown in Figure 5.6. In other words, Catholics in Wales were less likely to be Eurosceptic than those elsewhere in Britain. While the small sample of Catholics in Wales in the BESIP prohibits any further analysis or interrogation of this finding, it does suggest the possibility that Catholicism is not as unified – in terms of its impact on political attitudes – as is commonly assumed. This suggestion is reinforced by the tendency of Catholics in Scotland to be (slightly) more left-wing than non-Catholics – a trait not replicated in England or Wales.

Just as important as the significant effects are those anticipated effects our analyses did not find. There were no significant effects on Euroscepticism stemming from identifying as Baptist or Methodist, anywhere in Britain. They were no more or less likely to identify as European or hold any other national identity; no more likely to be economically right- or left-wing; and no more likely to be socially conservative. This is not to say that identifying with such communities has no political consequences at all. Baptists in Wales, for example, were found to be more slightly likely to identify as Welsh and to support Plaid Cymru – but no such effects were significantly related to being Eurosceptic or any of the mediating characteristics in between.

A further surprise was the absence of any evidence of a substantial effect from religious behaviour. We did find that more religiously active people in Scotland were slightly more likely to be economically right-wing, which led them to be more likely to identify with the Conservatives and so increased their AES, but this effect was very weak. Not only did we not find religious behaviour affecting tolerance for migration (as expected), but we found no relationship between religious behaviour or any other mediating trait, nor any direct effect on either dimension of Euroscepticism. This is a puzzling finding: while it is plausible that even if religious behaviour increases social capital it may not lead to greater tolerance for immigration and so less Eurosceptic attitudes, we would still expect to find a relationship between religious behaviour and Euroscepticism given the consistent finding – not just in previous chapters but previous research (e.g. Boomgaarden and Freire 2009; McAndrew 2020) – that religious behaviour depresses Euroscepticism. There is little question that people who are more religiously active are less likely to express Eurosceptic attitudes or vote in Eurosceptic ways when given the opportunity – Chapters 3 and 4 both demonstrate as much. The fact that we find no relationship between the two at all in the SEMs, however, raises the possibility that religious behaviour does not depress Euroscepticism but is rather closely correlated with another characteristic that does so but is not present in our analysis. Another possibility is that this is an artefact of our data or methodology; something perhaps specific to the context of the UK's 2016 referendum (although McAndrew's 2020 research disputes this) or the SEMs (although Boomgaarden and Freire 2009 used a similar method). A further possibility is that this reflects our choice of dependent variable: while the religiously active are less likely to vote against EC/EU membership or express dissatisfaction with it, when asked questions tapping into their views of European integration without implying a change or termination of membership they may become more critical and/or their positions diverge. Further research is required to explain this puzzling finding and doing so identifies an important avenue of further inquiry. For now, all we can conclude is that while the more religiously active were more likely to oppose Brexit in 2016 (see Chapter 4), we can find no evidence that this was because they were less likely to be Eurosceptic or more tolerant of migration.

Finally, to get an idea of the magnitude of these multiple religious effects, we present a summary of the combined indirect effects of the three religious identities that affected Euroscepticism – Anglicanism, Presbyterianism and Catholicism – in Table 5.1.

The indirect effects are calculated by multiplying the coefficients for each pathway along the causal relationship of interest and then summing the totals (Boomgaarden and Freire 2009). The table also estimates the combined effect of each identity on Euroscepticism by summing the total effects on AES and UES. None of the resulting religious effects could be described as strong – at most, religious identity had a moderate effect on Euroscepticism. The two religious communities that were substantially more likely to be Eurosceptic in the Brexit referendum were Anglicans in England and Presbyterians in Scotland. While Catholics in England and Scotland were also more likely to be Eurosceptic, the effect was weak (and, as Chapter 4 showed, this was offset by the fact that most Catholics were religiously active). Only one religious community was less likely to be Eurosceptic, which was Catholics in Wales, but again the effect was weak. Before the

Table 5.1 Total standardised effect of religion on Euroscepticism

England	
Anglican → UES	0.15
Anglican → AES	0.18
Anglican → ES	0.33
Catholic → UES	0.03
Catholic → AES	0.03
Catholic → ES	0.06
Scotland	
Catholic → UES	0.04
Catholic → AES	0.04
Catholic → ES	0.08
Presbyterian → UES	0.16
Presbyterian → AES	0.18
Presbyterian → ES	0.34
Attendance → AES	0.01
Wales	
Anglican → UES	0.09
Anglican → AES	0.18
Anglican → ES	0.27
Catholic → UES	−0.06
Catholic → AES	−0.06
Catholic → ES	−0.12

Source: BESIP. Standardised coefficients calculated using STATA

importance of religion is dismissed, however, it should be borne in mind that, first, when talking about those who's Anglican identity predisposed them to be more Eurosceptic, we are referring to over a fifth of British adults. Second, this analysis only focused on identifying the causal roots through which religion affected Euroscepticism: as was shown in Chapter 4, there is evidence that some 'religious effects' can be substantial once the impact of religious behaviour, belief and belonging are considered simultaneously. While we could find no significant effect from religious behaviour on Euroscepticism or the mediator variables in this analysis to explain this, this does neither change the fact that more religiously active voters were significantly less likely to support Brexit in 2016 or be Eurosceptic in the 40 years before, nor that the difference between some religiously active voters (such as Catholics) and some religiously inactive voters (such as Anglicans) was substantial.

Summary and conclusion

When we speak of religion and Euroscepticism in Britain, these analyses show that we are essentially talking about two groups of religious voters, and both are more Eurosceptic because of their religious identities: national church Protestants and Catholics. Whether Anglicans in England or Presbyterians in Scotland, national church Protestants exhibit a range of characteristics that make them significantly less likely to support the principle of European integration and more critical of the costs and benefits associated with EU membership. Principally, this includes their propensity to be socially conservative, to reject a transnational European identity and (in the case of Anglicans) to hold an English national identity. These not only directly increase their hostility towards the EU but also make them more critical of the migration associated with EU membership, in terms of both its economic and cultural impact, which further undermines support for integration. National church Protestants also exhibit a tendency to be more right-wing: this also contributes to their Euroscepticism, but its influence is far weaker (and for Presbyterians, is limited to increasing their likelihood of identifying with the Conservatives). The other group are Catholics, who – at least in England and Scotland – are also more likely to be socially conservative. This similarly makes them more critical of the principle of integration as well as the benefits of membership and more likely to be hostile towards migration. Catholics' social conservatism is not as pronounced, however, as that of national church Protestants, and they also do not exhibit the same national identities. While Catholics are more Eurosceptic than non-Catholics, therefore, they are not quite so critical of the EU as Anglicans or Presbyterians.

Free church Protestantism, on the other hand, is not related in any substantial way to Euroscepticism. This not only undermines the frequent claim in previous research that Protestantism promotes Euroscepticism – that only being true for national church Protestants – but also many of the ideological characteristics frequently attributed to Christian voters regardless of their denomination. We found no greater than average tendency for Baptists or Methodists to be socially conservative, economically right- or left-wing, or to adopt or reject the European national identity. This is not to say that such religious communities have no distinctive political characteristics – examples of such distinctions are provided in the next chapter – simply that none of those characteristics result in them being unusually supportive or critical of EU membership. Perhaps the most important conclusion of this chapter as far as free church Protestantism is concerned is that it is essential that future studies of Protestant political characteristics do not treat all Protestant communities as a homogenous group. Doing so not only misrepresents the political characteristics of free church Protestants, but also biases estimates of those characteristics among other Protestant groups as well. If Anglicans, Baptists and Methodists were treated as a single Protestant category in this research, for example, we would conclude that Anglicans are far less Eurosceptic than they actually are. As argued by Kolpinskaya and Fox (2019), the very theories that are used to explain why Protestants are more Eurosceptic than Catholics, give plenty of reason to believe that national church and free church Protestants would differ in their political attitudes: they have distinct historical experiences of engagement with the Catholic and national churches and have far weaker relationships than the latter with nation states, national governments and conceptions of national identity. While it is not always possible to study distinct Protestant groups in social surveys that typically include very small numbers of such communities, at the very least national church Protestants should be separated from 'other Protestants'.

The findings of this chapter challenge many of the established theories of religion and Euroscepticism in the current literature. As discussed earlier, one such challenge is the assumption that Protestants are essentially homogenous when it comes to their views of European integration. Another, also discussed in Chapter 4, is that Catholicism depresses Euroscepticism because of the overlap between European integration and the political structure advocated by the Catholic Church, and the links between Catholicism and a transnational identity. Our analyses have repeatedly shown that this is not the case: Catholicism, to the extent that it affects Euroscepticism at all, increases hostility towards the EU because it is associated with a more socially conservative outlook and subsequently more critical views of immigration. The anti-Brexit views of most Catholics, as we showed in Chapter 4, stem from their far greater tendency to be religiously active than national church Protestants. This is not to say that country-level effects – in

Untangling (in)direct effects of religion on Euroscepticism 89

which people living in historically Catholic countries are likely to have been raised in a culture that promotes some Catholic values which may be sympathetic to European integration – do not exist (Scherer 2020; Nelsen and Guth 2015; Boomgaarden and Freire 2009), but it does suggest that the individual-level relationship explaining those effects (i.e. being socialised into a society exhibiting more Catholic values) may need further examination given that no such effect is found at the individual level in this study. That said, a further important finding from the SEMs above is evidence of a distinction in political attitudes between Catholics in England, Scotland and Wales. While the differences are small, we found that Catholics in Wales tended to be slightly more pro-EU than non-Catholics, while those in England and Scotland tended to be more Eurosceptic, and that the consequences of Catholicism – in terms of social conservatism, left-right ideology and a European identity – were somewhat different in each country. While these differences were small and caution has to be employed when looking into differences between what are small samples of survey respondents, this is nonetheless evidence that Catholicism exhibits a different political character in different regions or countries, one that must also be effectively accounted for to avoid misrepresentations of their political traits. Further research, with a considerably larger sample of Catholics than is available to us, would be required to explore this further and effectively theorise why Catholicism may evoke differing political characteristics in different regions, countries or communities. Such a study constitutes a potentially enlightening step forward in understanding the political consequences of identifying with the – or perhaps that should read one of the – Catholic communities.

The final consideration of this chapter is what the use of distinct dimensions of Euroscepticism reveal about the relationship between it and religion. Interestingly, the analyses showed that – with the exception of Anglicanism in Wales, the effect of which on AES was roughly twice as strong as that on UES – the consequences of national church Protestantism and Catholicism are broadly similar: such communities are more likely to oppose the principle of European integration and to view the consequences of EU membership in a more critical light as a result of their religious values and identities. While the most important consequences of religious identity for Euroscepticism are increased social conservatism and (for national church Protestants) a rejection of transnational identities (coupled with holding a strong English identity for Anglicans), these have similar impacts on both UES and AES. In other words, the communitarian values and attachments to traditional social and political institutions, prioritisation of authority and stability over freedom of expression, and exclusive national identities of Anglicans and Presbyterians make them more likely both to oppose the principle of European integration – as it undermines many of those institutions and invites strong pressures for change through mass migration – and to be critical of the consequences of EU membership – as it undermines the prosperity of their communities. Among Catholics (outside Wales), it is their social conservatism that matters and produces similar consequences (though to a lesser extent). This suggests that at least some of the Euroscepticism of national church Protestants and Catholics could be reduced if they were to perceive the consequences of EU membership to be more beneficial. As noted in Chapter 2, it is possible that the increasingly secular and socially liberal direction of European integration and policy is affecting the support of Christian communities for the process. While we lack the data to verify that this is part of the explanation for the UES of Anglicans, Presbyterians and Catholics, it is certainly plausible. On the other hand, such efforts will only ever meet with limited success because another part of their Euroscepticism is rooted in firm opposition to the principle of European integration and the perception that the authority of European institutions is illegitimate and/or inappropriately exercised. To the extent that there is any policy response that could address such scepticism, it is likely to be that already enacted in the UK: withdrawal from the EU.

Text Box 5.1 SEM development

SEM analysis involves two stages: a model development stage and a results stage. In fields where causal relationships are not particularly well understood or empirical testing of those relationships is limited (such as religion and Euroscepticism), we cannot simply apply a theoretically derived model to our data and interpret the results. The model may not fit the data, and if that is the case estimates for how variables are related could be biased (they may not be, of course; the point is that we would have no way of knowing). We can only meaningfully interpret results and test theories, therefore, using a model that we are confident provides a satisfactory representation of how the variables are related in the dataset. This means building a SEM that represents theoretical expectations (as in Figure 5.2) and testing its fit, then modifying it until the best fitting and theoretically coherent model is identified. The details of our model development are not presented here for the sake of brevity and because the substantive results of the SEM are of greater importance, but they are available from the authors on request.

Notes

1 Respondents were invited to say they were 'not religious' when asked how religiously active they were; we interpret this as them offering an explanation for not engaging in religious activity at all.
2 To test the validity of these measurement models, we used Mokken Scale Analysis, the full details of which are reported in Online Appendix.
3 Our SEM assumes that AES and UES, while co-varying, are independent. This is a questionable assumption, as there could easily be causal effects between them: people who feel that the EU consistently fails to achieve its policy objectives, or that Member State lose more than they gain from EU membership, could well come to question the legitimacy of the institution (i.e. UES causing AES). Similarly, people who feel that the EU is an illegitimate or corrupt institution could easily conclude that it provides no material benefits to their country (i.e. AES causing UES). Testing such theories would require multiple consecutive waves of BESIP data on Euroscepticism, which are not available, as well as an array of additional analyses that are beyond the scope of this research. Even if the two are causally related, however, it should have no substantial effect on our estimates of how they are related to religion.
4 All the SEMs were produced using Stata 14 and maximum likelihood estimation. The data were weighted using BESIP panel weights.

6 Cushioning the blow
Religion and party politics in the age of Brexit

> Much psephological blood has been spilled on the question of whether religion or class is the most important influence on voting in contemporary democracies.
>
> Harrop and Miller (1987: 177)

The impact of the Brexit referendum on Britain's politics was as dramatic as its result was unexpected. Within 24 hours of the result, the Prime Minister resigned and a no confidence motion was tabled in the Leader of the Opposition. Within a year, Prime Minister Theresa May announced her intention to hold a general election to 'guarantee certainty for the years ahead' and strengthen the government's position ahead of its negotiations with the EU (BBC 2017). The outcome of the election was anything but certainty – a 'hung' parliament that paralysed government and left the question of whether the UK would leave the EU open for two more years. In 2019, Theresa May was replaced by one of the leaders of the Vote Leave campaign, Boris Johnson, whose own inability to deliver Brexit led him to demand the third general election in four years. This time the outcome was far more favourable to supporters of Brexit – a stunning 80-seat Conservative majority. Fifty days later, the UK left the EU.

The results of the 2017 and 2019 general elections were remarkable for several reasons. The 2017 election saw substantial increases in support for both the major parties, who successfully appealed to the majority of voters on either side of the Brexit divide at the expense of the smaller parties, whereby the Conservatives monopolised the pro-Brexit vote, and Labour the Remain vote (Cowley and Kavanagh 2018; Fieldhouse et al. 2020). The Conservatives' victory in 2019 was built on their continued success in winning over pro-Brexit constituencies in former Labour heartlands, while Labour was unable to win enough constituencies more sympathetic to EU membership to compensate and the party fell to its worst result for decades (Cutts et al. 2019; Ford 2019; Fisher 2020).

Cushioning the blow   93

The transformation of Labour and Conservative support after 2016 was another consequence of the gradual changes in the priorities of British voters – and their connections to their political parties – that started 40 years earlier and were accelerated by the 'electoral shock' of Brexit (discussed in Chapter 1). Voters' loyalties to political parties – and the social institutions upon which those parties' formation was based (including religion and social class) – had weakened, and they were more prepared to switch votes between elections depending on who best represented their agenda. Their political priorities had changed, with deference to authority and traditional institutions, freedom of expression, individual autonomy, national identity, communitarianism and internationalism more important than since at least the 1975 referendum, and the left/right economic divide less central to the outcome of elections (Fieldhouse et al. 2020; Ford and Goodwin 2017; Evans and Menon 2017; Sobolewska and Ford 2020). Those socially conservative, communitarian voters with exclusive (primarily English) national identities who opposed European integration and immigration found themselves largely ignored (by the Conservatives) or taken for granted (by Labour) in the 2000s and were particularly receptive to the messages of the BNP and the UKIP – with their support for the latter helping to pressure David Cameron into promising the EU referendum in the first place. After the referendum, both major parties dramatically revised their agendas to react to what their leaders believed was an 'antiestablishment vote' and a 'vote for serious change' (Shipman 2017). While this was also driven by the agendas the relatively new leaders of each party wanted to pursue (particularly, Labour under Jeremy Corbyn), both parties quickly abandoned any support for EU membership and embraced a distinctly pro-Brexit platform in the 2017 election (Labour Party 2017; Conservative Party 2017).

The Conservatives maintained their explicitly pro-Brexit stance in both the 2017 and 2019 elections, as well as promoting sceptical views of immigration and tougher approaches on law and order, as they set out to win over the 'more nationalistic, communitarian and inward-looking' sections of the electorate who overwhelmingly endorsed Brexit (Ford and Goodwin 2017: 19). The party successfully appealed to swathes of older, working-class, socially conservative voters who for years had constituted the core of Labour's working-class support. Despite their Brexit policy in 2017 being virtually identical to that of the Conservatives, Labour took a far more critical view of it and even promised a second referendum including a 'Remain' option on the ballot in its 2019 manifesto. Despite dissenting voices from MPs representing northern former industrial constituencies, the party focused on the younger, university educated voters who '[regard] diversity as a core social strength; discrimination by gender, race, religion or sexual orientation as a key social evil . . . national identity as a matter of civic attachment . . . [and think] that individual freedoms matter much more than communal values' (Ford and Goodwin 2017: 19; Pogrund and Maguire 2020). Such voters overwhelmingly supported Jeremy Corbyn's leadership of the Labour Party in 2015, opposed Brexit in 2016 and had long seen immigration as a social benefit. In both 2017 and 2019, Labour successfully won the support of this constituency. Its catastrophic result in the latter election stemmed from the party's (understandable) failure to escape the impossible position of its support, while based largely on former Remain voters, including a sizeable majority of pro-Brexit voters concentrated in so-called 'red wall' constituencies that were far more receptive to Boris Johnson's 'Get Brexit Done' campaign than the muddled second referendum promise of Jeremy Corbyn (Cutts et al. 2019).

The contribution of religion to this process has been mostly explored by focusing on the effects of secularisation. Fieldhouse et al. (2020) and de Geus and Shorrocks (2020) show that secularisation contributed to younger generations becoming less conservative and less loyal to political parties, because of their lack of attachment to a religious community with the accompanying social conservatism and historic partisan predisposition. As we noted in Chapter 1, however, the assumption that secularisation has led to religion being all but irrelevant in shaping voter behaviour is misguided. Tilley (2015) shows that religion continues to shape voter behaviour to this day, even among those who do not identify with religious communities, because of the political habits and loyalties that are passed on from older generations. Along with McAndrew (2017a), Tilley also shows that voters who identify with religious communities continue to exhibit partisan preferences for the traditional party of those communities, rooted in the historic relationships between them formed decades ago.

In our final chapter, we build on and extend these studies to examine the voting behaviour of the largest Christian communities in Britain between the 1979 and 2019 general elections (i.e. throughout the UK's EC/EU membership), and how it has changed over time in light of the rising salience of Euroscepticism and social conservatism and the changing nature of British party politics (such as in light of the rise of UKIP in the 2000s). We then look at the role of religion in explaining voter behaviour specifically in the post-referendum period, assessing both its impact in driving or frustrating changes in party loyalty reflecting voters' preferences on Brexit and the continued importance of religion to explaining UK election results. This chapter makes two key arguments. Firstly, in line with Tilley (2015), we show that religion – specifically, religious belonging – continues to influence voting behaviour among British Christians, and that the changes in voter loyalty and behaviour associated with the rise of Euroscepticism and social conservatism since the 1980s also led to changes in the partisan loyalties of the religious communities. This trend has been accelerated by Brexit and has resulted in the divergence in religious voting that characterised British elections throughout the 20th century – in which Anglicans and Presbyterians were disproportionately likely to vote Conservative while Catholics were more likely to vote Labour – being replaced by a tendency for Christians to increasingly support the Conservatives. Our final argument, therefore, is that while it certainly did not cause this change, Brexit and Euroscepticism have contributed to a change in the British party system which sees the Conservative Party emerge as the closest British politics has ever seen to a Christian Democratic Party.

Religion and voting in Britain before and after Brexit

The origin of the 'Christian vote'

While the influence of religion in British politics and on party support has been declining since World War II, Britain's Christian communities have long maintained a propensity to support one or another political party. This is not because of overlap between their religious values and party ideologies. Steven (2010) points out that the ideological priorities of Christians are apparent within the agendas of all the major parties. Rather, it reflects the historic relationships between the Christian communities and the major parties, and the predisposition to support those parties instilled within members of those communities, frequently through early socialisation (Tilley 2015). Hence, it is voters' attachment to religious communities (religious belonging) that lies at the heart of Britain's Christian 'religious vote'.

Anglicans and Presbyterians have long favoured the Conservative Party because of its support for the historically privileged position of the Church of England and the Presbyterian Church of Scotland within the British state and government. Indeed, for much of the 16th and 17th centuries the Church of England and the English state were largely the same, with the church having enormous control over education, social behaviour, marriage and community infrastructure (McLean and Linsley 2004; Steven 2010). While this 'Anglican privilege' was opposed by Radicals, Liberals and 'non-conformists', it was protected by the Tory and then Conservative Party, with the Church of England frequently known as 'the Conservative Party at prayer' (Steven 2010: 67). The Conservatives' attachment to other traditional institutions supported by Anglicans and Presbyterians – including traditional conceptions of the family, marriage and national identity – as well as its opposition to Scottish separatism, have also underpinned the link between them.

Roman Catholics, on the other hand, have preferred the Labour Party since its emergence in the early 20th century. This partly reflects Catholic hostility to the Church of England and their persecution at its hands and that of the British state, leading them to support campaigners for radical change to the establishment (Steven 2010). It also reflects the ancestral and migrant origins of Britain's Catholic population, many of whom descended from Irish working-class migrants to England and Scotland in the 1940s and 1950s and who had roots in the Irish trade union movement, making Labour a natural home (Tilley 2015).

Finally, free church Protestants have, like Catholics, tended to support parties opposed to the Church of England (which persecuted them when they refused to conform to the Church's authority, hence the derogatory label 'non-conformists') and the policies sympathetic to Anglican privilege within the British state (Steven 2010). Their institutional organisation – rooted in local communities with no overarching institutional authority – meant they also found the 'live and let live' ideology of classical liberalism appealing (McAndrew 2017a; Tilley 2015). In the 18–19th centuries, this saw free church Protestants primarily support the Liberal Party, and they continue to display sympathies for the Liberal Democrats (McAndrew 2017a). There are also links between Methodism and the emergence of Labour in the early 1900s – with many of Labour's early social policies drawn from Calvinist Methodists in Welsh industrialised communities (McLean and Linsley 2004).

The 'Christian vote' and EU membership

We used the BES to examine the voting behaviour of the Christian communities between the 1979 and 2019 general elections, covering almost the duration of the UK's EU membership.[1] As the primary source of religious voting in Britain (for Christians) is the historic relationships between the major parties and the Christian communities, and given the small sample sizes of particularly the earlier BES surveys, our focus is on religious belonging only. In Figures 6.1 and 6.2, we show the support of the Christian communities (as well as the non-religious for reference) for the Conservatives, Labour, Liberal Democrats and UKIP/Brexit Party. The data for Presbyterians are limited to Scotland, for which we also include the SNP. Figure 6.1 shows the (weighted) proportion of each community that supported each party between 1979 and 2019. To make it easier to identify the greater or lesser propensity of the communities to vote for the parties, Figure 6.2 shows the support of each community for each party net of their national vote.

Cushioning the blow 97

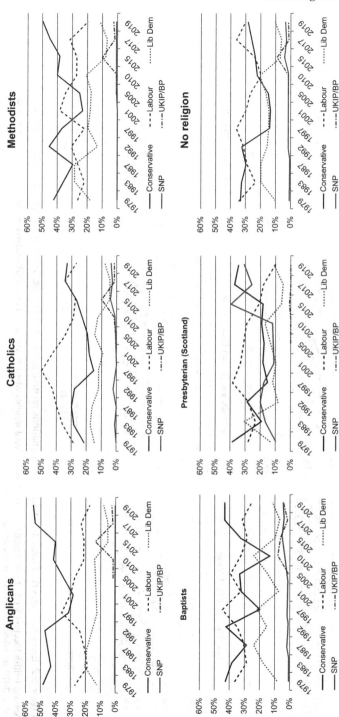

Figure 6.1 Voting behaviour of largest Christian denominations, 1979–2019 general elections, per cent

Source: British Election Study. Data weighted using cross-sectional weights where possible. Data for 1979–2010 come from post-election BES surveys, and data for 2015–2019 are taken from BESIP post-election waves

98 *Cushioning the blow*

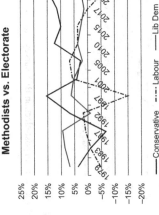

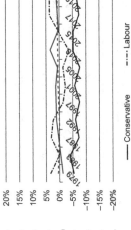

Figure 6.2 Electoral support of largest Christian denominations relative to wider electorate, 1979–2019 general elections, per cent

Source: British Election Study. Data weighted using cross-sectional weights where possible. Data for 1979–2010 come from post-election BES surveys, and data for 2015–2019 are taken from BESIP post-election waves

The data show a clear propensity for Anglicans and Presbyterians to exhibit above-average support for the Conservatives since the 1970s. In 1979, for example, almost half of Anglicans voted Tory, while 27 per cent voted Labour and 13 per cent Lib Dem. Between 1979 and 2001, even as support for the Conservatives in the wider electorate plummeted (particularly in 1997 and 2001) Anglican support remained around 9 points higher for the Tories than that of the wider electorate. Similarly, Presbyterian support for the Conservatives in Scotland was on average 7 points higher than that of the wider electorate between 1979 and 2015. Even though on several occasions more Presbyterians voted Labour than Conservative, they nonetheless exhibited a greater propensity to vote Tory than the wider Scottish electorate. Moreover, both established church Protestant communities have become even more likely to vote Conservative in recent years. After 2001, the gap between Anglican and the wider electorate's support for the Tories grew, reaching 12 points in 2005 and 14 in 2010, before falling slightly to 12 in 2015 (after David Cameron's socially liberal coalition government was in office, during which time same-sex marriage was legalised against the objections of many Conservative Party members and supporters). After Brexit, the Tories' 'Anglican boost' grew to 20 points in 2017 and 2019. In Scotland, their 'Presbyterian boost' increased to 15 points in 2017, before falling to 11 points in 2019 (though this was still higher than the pre-2015 average). As we would expect, given the tendency of Anglicans and Presbyterians to be more supportive of Brexit, both communities were given more of a reason to vote Conservative after the EU referendum when the issue of Brexit (and the values associated with Euroscepticism) topped the political agenda. Another interesting feature of Presbyterian voting is their support for the Liberal Democrats. They showed a marginally greater propensity to support the Lib Dems after the 1980s (when Scotland as a whole all but rejected the Margaret Thatcher's governments and the Conservative Party) – with their net support for the party around 1 point higher on average than that of the Scottish electorate. Figure 6.2 also shows that Presbyterians – despite being more likely than non-Presbyterians to hold a Scottish national identity (see Chapter 5) – were no more or less likely to support the SNP (except for a small and brief increase between 1992 and 1997). This is perhaps surprising given most Presbyterians' opposition to Scottish separatism (Tilley 2015).

The greater propensity of Catholics to support Labour is clear in both Figures 6.1 and 6.2. Equally clear, however, is a precipitous decline in Labour's Catholic vote since the early 1990s. In 1983, for example, when Labour suffered one of the worst results of its history, Catholic support for the party was 13 points higher than that of the wider electorate, and it increased to 14 points in 1987 and 1992. From 1997, it started to deteriorate, dropping to 10 points

100 *Cushioning the blow*

in 2001, 5 points in 2010 and 4 points in 2015. By the 2019 election, it had disappeared entirely. At the same time, Catholic hostility to the Conservatives has been softening. In 1979, Catholic support for the Conservatives was 17 points lower than in the wider electorate and averaged 9 points lower than the electorate between 1983 and 1992. This gap fell to 7 points in 1997 and 3 points between 2005 and 2015. By 2019, Catholic support for the Conservatives was 2 points *higher* than that of the wider electorate. This is particularly surprising given that most Catholics (as we saw in Chapter 3) were opposed to Brexit, which should, if anything, have given them more of a reason to support Labour. Instead, more Catholics voted Conservative in 2019 than Labour for the first time since at least 1979. Labour's collapse of Catholic support mirrors the decline in Labour's working-class support described by Evans and Tilley (2017) – although it begins earlier than the process they describe – and may well be a result of the same process given that most Catholics in Britain in the 1980–2000s were from working-class backgrounds.

The data for Baptists and Methodists must be interpreted with slightly more caution because of their small numbers in any individual BES survey, making fluctuations from one election to the next that reflect nothing more than statistical noise more likely. Two broad trends are nonetheless discernible. First, consistent with the expectation above, while most have supported either Labour or the Conservatives in any given election, Methodists have been more supportive of Liberal Democrats than the wider electorate – with their support for the party 5 points higher on average between 1979 and 2015. Methodists are also equally likely to support the Conservatives – with their support for the Tories also around 5 points higher than the wider electorate. Remarkably, there is no evidence of any 'Methodist boost' for Labour since 1979. Baptists, on the other hand, have been more supportive of Labour – with their support averaging 6 points higher than that of the electorate between 1979 and 2015. Whereas they have also leaned towards the Liberal Democrats, their support was only 1 point higher on average. The graphs also show that the voting behaviour of free church Protestants is changing. Figure 6.1 shows a plurality of Methodists and Baptists voted Conservative in 2017 and 2019, while support for Labour fell and support for the Lib Dems stagnated at the 2015 level. The Conservatives' support amongst Methodists, by contrast, increased relative to the wider electorate from 10 points in 2015 to 14 points in 2019, while their Baptist support relative to the wider electorate increased from 4 points higher in 2015 to 8 points higher in 2019.

A Brexit effect?

We do not have the data to definitively identify the source of this shift away from Labour towards the Conservatives among Britain's Christian voters.

It is certainly consistent, however, with what we would expect given the increasing salience of Euroscepticism, national identity and social conservatism as determinants of public opinion and voter behaviour since the 1980s – with the social conservatism of Anglicans, Presbyterians and Catholics, in particular, making them more likely to support the more socially conservative of the two major parties. We can get some insight into the role Euroscepticism might have played by looking at the more recent elections for which sufficient data is available. In Figure 6.3, we look at how religion and Brexit influenced changes in voter behaviour between the 2015 and 2019 elections using data from the BESIP panel. Focusing on the major parties only, we show each religious groups' support for Labour and the Conservatives, as well as the SNP in Scotland, depending on whether they supported or opposed the UK's withdrawal from the EU in 2015.

For the most part, changes in religious party voting after 2015 were small – there are no indications of dramatic shifts induced by Brexit. On the contrary, we see evidence of religion acting as a 'buffer' against such realignments, as the historic links between religious communities and their political parties made defections less likely. Anglicans and Presbyterians who opposed Brexit in 2016, for example, were unusually likely to support the Conservatives in 2017 and 2019. Support for the Tories was on average 14 points higher among Anglican Remainers than Remainers in the wider electorate, but only 9 points higher among Anglican Brexiteers compared with the Brexiteer electorate. Similarly, among Presbyterians in Scotland, Conservative support was 8 points higher among Presbyterian Remainers and only 3 points higher among Presbyterian Brexiteers, than their counterparts in the wider electorate. At the same time, both Anglicans and Presbyterians were less likely than the wider electorate to support Labour, particularly if they were opposed to Brexit. Remainer Anglican support for Labour was 10 points lower than Remainer non-Anglican support in 2017 and 5 points lower in 2019, while for Presbyterians these figures were 3 points and 7 point, respectively. This does not mean that more anti-Brexit Anglicans or Presbyterians voted Conservative than pro-Brexit Anglicans. In fact, Conservative support among Remainer Anglicans fell in all three elections, from 39 per cent in 2015 to 36 per cent in 2017 and 20 per cent in 2019. Moreover, in 2019 more Remain-supporting Anglicans voted Labour (42 per cent) than Conservative. It does mean, however, that even as critics of Brexit were abandoning the Conservatives after 2015, Anglicans opposed to Brexit were less likely to do so.

There were few differences after 2015 between Catholics and the wider electorate, regardless of their support for Brexit, reflecting the steady erosion of a clear Catholic party preference identified earlier. The one exception is pro-Brexit Catholics' support for the Conservatives, which was unusually

102 *Cushioning the blow*

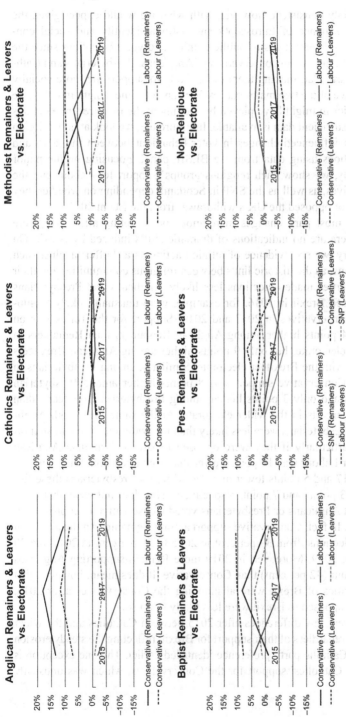

Figure 6.3 Change in relative support of religious voters by support for Brexit, per cent
Source: BESIP. Data weighted using cross-sectional weights

low, at 4 points below the wider pro-Brexit electorate. This may reflect Catholics' historic suspicion of the party. The fact that there was no greater propensity for Catholics to vote Labour, however, even among those opposed to Brexit, is remarkable. In an election seemingly dominated by Brexit, we might expect a Catholic Remainer to have few reasons not to vote for the party. They evidently found some, however, and this further illustrates just how dramatic the collapse in Labour's Catholic support has been.

Finally, small samples once again mean interpreting data for Methodists and Baptists is hazardous. While there were greater tendencies among Methodist Remainers and Baptist Brexiteers to support Labour and among Baptist Remainers to vote Conservative, these were small and short-lived. Two more stable tendencies are apparent, however. The first is that Methodist Remainers exhibited above-average support for the Conservatives in all three elections – with their vote being 6 points higher on average than among Remainers in the wider electorate. The second is the tendency of pro-Brexit Baptists and Methodists to vote Conservative in greater numbers than among the wider pro-Brexit electorate. In all three elections, for example, the Conservative vote was on average 9 points higher among Brexiter Methodists and 10 points higher among Brexiter Baptists, than among Brexiteers in the electorate. This represents a continuation of the trend for free church Protestants to have become more likely to vote Conservative, but also shows the trend accelerated among those who supported Brexit. As with Anglicans and Presbyterians, it is likely that the Conservatives' staunch support for Brexit and their socially conservative stances on immigration and law and order appealed to those Eurosceptic Baptists and Methodists.

Conclusion

In their seminal study of voting behaviour in Britain after the EU referendum, Fieldhouse et al. (2020: 27) showed that British politics has become characterised by unprecedented volatility, in which '[m]ore voters are switching their vote choices than ever', and as a result 'British politics has become less predictable and the party system less stable'. At least part of the reason for this was secularisation, whereby the growing number of voters without a religious identification meant a larger proportion of the British electorate lacking a link with the Conservatives (for Anglicans and Presbyterians), Labour (for Catholics) or the Liberal Democrats (for Methodists or Baptists) that would make them more likely to vote for that party even if an electoral shock such as Brexit encouraged them to shift their party loyalties.

Our analyses show that there remain clear religious effects in voting post-Brexit, with clear differences in support for political parties that reflect the historic relationships between those parties and the Anglican, Presbyterian,

Catholic and free church communities. Anglicans and Presbyterians, for example, have exhibited above-average support for the Conservatives over the last 40 years, while Methodists have expressed more support for the Liberal Democrats and Catholics – at least in the 1980s – were more likely to vote for Labour. We also find, however, that the relationship between Britain's largest Christian communities and its political parties is changing. It is evolving and, in some cases, reinforcing the traditional links between those communities and parties, while in others eroding them. The overarching nature of the trend is a shift away from Labour and the Liberal Democrats and towards the Conservatives: for Anglicans and Presbyterians, this represents a strengthening of the historic ties with their 'traditional party'; for free church Protestants, it represents a steady shift away from Labour or the Liberal Democrats towards the Conservatives; and among Catholics it represents a far more dramatic collapse in support for Labour. There is also evidence of the traditional connections between religious communities and political parties acting as a 'buffer' against the dramatic realignment in party support following the 2016 referendum. While pro-Brexit voters were likely to shift from Labour to the Conservatives and anti-Brexit voters shifted from the Conservatives to Labour or the SNP, those that identified with religious communities were less likely to defect if it meant abandoning their 'traditional party'. This saw anti-Brexit Anglicans and Presbyterians being less likely to switch from the Tories than other anti-Brexit voters, and pro-Brexit Catholics less likely to embrace the Tories.

The objective of this chapter has been to examine the voting behaviour of Britain's Christian communities in light of the wider changes to the electorate throughout the UK's EC/EU membership and to look for evidence of Brexit affecting that behaviour; to that end, it has focused on descriptive statistics of Christian voting since 1979. In so doing, it has identified trends in religious voting that, to our knowledge, have not been identified or studied elsewhere. Employing the more sophisticated analyses and detailed data used in previous chapters is beyond the scope and objectives of this chapter, and as such we are less able to explain the trends we identify here. We argue it is likely that the changes in voting behaviour among Britain's Christian communities are at least in part a result of the rising salience of Euroscepticism, national identity and social conservatism in public debate and as determinants of voters' priorities – and the trends we document are certainly consistent with that theory. We cannot rule out the likely influence of other factors, however. The trend could also reflect changes in policy priority, and the fact that Britain's Christian voters are increasingly a smaller, older section of the electorate, and that since the 2000s, the Conservatives have made championing the interests of older voters a priority (e.g. introducing the 'triple lock' on pensions and focusing welfare cuts on schemes targeted primarily at younger people during the coalition government). In this context, voting Conservative could be an increasingly rational thing to do for older voters throughout the 2000s and 2010s (Chrisp and Pearce 2019). Another possibility is that this reflects a life cycle effect, in which voters become increasingly small 'c' conservative as they get older and tend to vote for conservative political parties as a result (van der Eijk and Franklin 2009). Even without changes to the political landscape, we would expect the ageing British Christian community to become more sympathetic to the Conservative Party over time. While the influence of such effects is likely, we can be confident that the rise of Euroscepticism has played some role, in light of the extensive evidence presented in this book showing that voters' religion affects their views on the issue, and that presented elsewhere showing that Euroscepticism has become an increasingly key determinant of British voters' political priorities (Fieldhouse et al. 2020; Sobolewska and Ford 2020; Ford and Goodwin 2014; Clarke et al. 2017). Elaborating on this analysis and exploring the emergence of the Conservative Party as the closest thing Britain has ever seen to a Christian Democratic Party is a challenge for future research.

Note

1 We did not use data from BES in the 1960s because the way the survey measured religion changed substantially in 1979. The data for 2015, 2017 and 2019 came from BESIP Waves 6, 13 and 19, respectively.

7 Concluding thoughts

In this book, we have demonstrated the enduring relevance of religion in explaining attitudes to European integration in Britain. Despite the ongoing secularisation of British society, affiliation with religious groups, as well as religious practice and belief, continue to shape the political attitudes and allegiances of a significant part of the British population. While the importance of religion has undoubtedly declined throughout the post-war era and will continue to do so as fewer voters express religious characteristics, the enduring influence of those characteristics on more than half of the electorate and the narrow margin of some election results, not to mention the 2016 UK's referendum on the EU membership, mean it would be premature to declare that – to use Steve Bruce's (2002) assertion – 'God is dead' when it comes to British politics.

This research contributes to our understanding of how religion – in a multitude of forms – has affected and continues to affect attitudes towards European integration. We show that religion has been a small but substantial driving force behind British Euroscepticism and, eventually, the Brexit vote. This force stems primarily from the impact religious identification has on voters' national identity and political ideology – with national church Protestants in particular being likely to hold exclusive national identities, reject markers of a shared identity with those from Europe, and more right-wing and considerably more socially conservative than those in other religious communities (particularly, free church Protestants) and the religiously unaffiliated. All these effects result in an increasingly Eurosceptic outlook among Anglicans and Presbyterians in Britain, both of whom are more likely to oppose the principle of European integration and view the consequences of EU membership in a more negative light. Catholics, contrary to the common depiction of them as a pro-EU community because of the overlap between European integration and Catholic supranationalism, are similarly more socially conservative than the religiously unaffiliated and free church Protestants, resulting in them also being more likely to oppose

Concluding thoughts 107

the principle of European integration and view its consequences negatively. However, Catholic and Protestant effects can manifest at the country-level stemming from the religious history of European nations (Scherer 2020; Boomgaarden and Freire 2009; Nelsen and Guth 2015). Nonetheless the popular assertion that Catholicism increases support for EU membership at the individual level is not supported by this research. The reason Catholics tend to be less Eurosceptic than national church Protestants is that they are far more likely to be religiously active, and this has long had a negative effect on Euroscepticism.

Our conclusions have important implications for future research on how Euroscepticism is influenced and shaped by religious characteristics. One of the key features of our study compared with previous research in this field is our focus on depth at the expense of breadth. In other words, we provide more extensive and rigorous analyses of how religion affects Euroscepticism in Britain in order to learn something about the relationship between the two in other contexts. While it is not possible to replicate our approach using multi-national datasets, it could be replicated in multiple national contexts using the wealth of survey data available in those countries with long histories of social survey research (such as Germany or the Netherlands). An important step for future research is comparing our findings with those in other countries based on similarly detailed approaches to confirm just how much of what we have shown here is generalisable to other European contexts. Even without such a study, however, our findings cast doubt on the validity of treating all Protestant communities as essentially homogenous in future analyses of their Eurosceptic attitudes. While doing so is an understandable response to small samples of differing Protestant communities in multi-national social surveys, our research shows that it (a) underestimates just how Eurosceptic some Protestants are – namely, those connected to the national or established church and (b) overestimates the Euroscepticism of Protestants without such connections. Moreover, without distinguishing between Protestant communities in our SEMs in Chapter 5, we would have been unable to identify the differences between them (in terms of national identity and political ideology) that accounted for their distinct positions on Europe. We also found evidence of a related distinction that is worthy of further study, that is, that between Catholic communities in different countries and/or communities. Most research (including our own) tends to view Catholics as a homogenous religious community, one that transcends national borders; indeed, association with such a community is a key defining feature of Catholicism (Nelsen and Guth 2015). In Chapter 5, however, we found evidence that Welsh Catholics' attitudes to Europe differed from those of Catholics in Scotland and England, because they were more left-wing and more likely to accept a European national identity. This raises the question of whether Catholicism is, at least in terms of political attitudes, more varied than frequently assumed along geographic terms.

Our research also highlights the importance of recognising the differing dimensions of religion when studying how it affects political attitudes in general. Along with numerous other studies (including McAndrew 2020; Clements 2015; Boomgaarden and Freire 2009; Ben-Nun Bloom and Arikan 2012, 2013), our analyses have consistently shown that religious belonging, behaviour and belief have distinct and independent effects on Euroscepticism. Failure to account for these multiple effects would not only lead to a mischaracterisation of how religion affects political attitudes, but also underestimate the potential magnitude of that impact. In Chapter 4, for example, we showed that while the effect of religious belief and belonging on their own were small relative to other traits that influence support for Brexit (such as age), their cumulative impact was in some cases considerable.

Finally, one of the most important contributions of this research is the use of structural equation modelling and panel data to test causal theories about how religious belonging and behaviour affect Euroscepticism. It is our use of such tools in Chapter 5 that confirms that religious belonging does affect Euroscepticism through its impact on national identity and political ideology; that this effect is limited to national church but not free church Protestants; that it has a substantial effect on political attitudes; and that Catholicism is associated with more – not less – Euroscepticism.

As we have discussed earlier, all these conclusions have substantial implications for existing theories about how religion affects Euroscepticism and constitute the most important contribution of this book to that field. Such a contribution would be impossible through the cross-sectional surveys and reliance on descriptive statistics and linear regression analysis that dominates research in the field, primarily because such tools cannot identify the multiple, indirect effects of religion on Euroscepticism. The only way of attempting to account for the effect of religion on traits such as national identity, political ideology and attitudes towards immigration in a regression model is to control for such variables when estimating the effect of religion. However, such variables are frequently unavailable in multi-national cross-sectional surveys, and simply controlling for them will not capture the relationship between them and religion but rather misrepresent the effect of both religion and the mediator variables on Euroscepticism. It is notable that stand-out studies that have explored the relationship between religion and Euroscepticism using panel data and/or methods such as structural equation modelling – such as this book, Kolpinskaya and Fox (2019), McAndrew (2020) and Boomgaarden and Freire (2009) – have all challenged existing theories regarding that relationship that are frequently employed in the

Concluding thoughts 109

literature. This research demonstrates the need for far greater use of panel data and statistical methods better suited to testing complex causal theories in research on the effects of religion on not just Euroscepticism but political attitudes and behaviour more broadly.

While such tools will help resolve many complex disputes about those relationships, one of the biggest challenges stemming from our results is the effect of religious behaviour. In analyses of data from the early 2000s, we find evidence of religious practice depressing Euroscepticism, in line with previous research (e.g. Smith and Woodhead 2018; McAndrew 2020). As we detailed in Chapter 2, this is expected to stem from the effect of elite cues (i.e. pro-EU messaging by religious leaders) and social capital (i.e. stronger sense of identity that reduces the perception of threat from deeper European integration). While these explanations are plausible, such causal relationships have not been established empirically considering the challenges of measuring causal effects in information flow models and the complexity of measuring social capital. Indeed, in SEMs, the relationship between attendance and Euroscepticism does not register as significant. While we would be hard pushed to argue one way or another considering such mixed evidence, it is crucial to highlight the importance of further research – both theoretical and empirical – with regard to how exactly (and why) religious attendance influences Euroscepticism. The fact that our study, McAndrew (2020) and Boomgaarden and Freire (2009) have reached different conclusions regarding the effects of religious behaviour and belonging further highlights the need to identify and explain the source of those differences and better understand the relationship between religious practice and Euroscepticism.

Our conclusions also have important implications for our understanding of British politics post-Brexit. As we discussed in Chapter 6, religion has long had an important effect on voting behaviour and partisan loyalty in Britain, the magnitude of which rivals that of social class. In showing that religious belonging affects national identity and political ideology (at least among Catholics and national church Protestants), we have shed light on the mechanism of that relationship and on its likely role in future years. Since the UK joined the EC, party politics has been increasingly affected by voters' priorities regarding socially conservative values – such as respect for traditional institutions, political and social stability, and authority over freedom of expression, and communitarianism – and national identity. Brexit did not create the deep divides between voters over such characteristics but created a context in which they could dominate political debate and unite those with similar priorities (such as social conservatives with a strong English national identity) around a single political cause. This conservative/liberal, nationalist/globalist ideological divide, as Maria Sobolewska and Rob Ford (2020) detail in their excellent book *Brexitland*, is here to stay and shape British politics beyond the outcomes of the recent general elections. In this context, the fact that religion has a stronger effect on social conservatism and national identity than on left/right economic values increases its salience for shaping voter priorities and behaviour for the foreseeable future.

It is particularly apparent in the voting behaviour of Britain's Christian communities. In Chapter 6, we showed how the traditional historic affiliations between those communities and the major political parties (i.e. Anglicans and Presbyterians disproportionately supporting the Conservatives, Catholics – Labour, free church Protestants – Labour and the Liberal Democrats) are being replaced by a growing tendency on the part of all Christian communities to reject the Labour Party and support the Conservatives. As the British electorate becomes more polarised along the lines of national identity and social conservatism versus cosmopolitanism and liberalism, rather than left versus right and/or social class divide, Britain's Christians have more reason than ever to support the parties that prioritise issues such as maintaining English national identity and traditional social and political institutions (namely, the Conservatives). This has contributed to the collapse of Labour's support among its 'traditional core vote' – white, working-class people in former industrial communities – and seen the Conservative Party emerge as the closest that Britain has ever had to a Christian Democratic Party in national politics. As British politics becomes increasingly polarised around social conservatism and national identity, and as Britain's Christian voters increasingly embrace the Conservatives to the detriment of Labour and the Liberal Democrats, this may result in religion playing a more prominent role in public debate as the 'religious vote' becomes a more important and unified constituency in the Conservative Party's electoral coalition.

Bibliography

Datasets

Fieldhouse, E., Green, J., Evans, G., Mellon, J. and Prosser, C. (2020) *British Election Study Internet Panel Wave 19*. Available at: www.britishelectionstudy.com/data-objects/panel-study-data/ [Accessed 24 August 2020].

Fieldhouse, E., Green, J., Evans, G., Schmitt, H., van der Eijk, C., Mellon, J. and Prosser, C. (2016) *British Election Study, 2015: Face-to-Face Post-Election Survey*, UK Data Service, SN: 7972. Available at: http://dx.doi.org/10.5255/UKDA-SN-7972-1 [Accessed 10 May 2019].

Fieldhouse, E., Green, J., Evans, G., Schmitt, H., van der Eijk, C., Mellon, J. and Prosser, C. (2019) *British Election Study, 2017: Face-to-Face Post-Election Survey*, UK Data Service, SN: 8418. Available at: http://doi.org/10.5255/UKDA-SN-8418-1 [Accessed 10 April 2020].

Heath, A., Curtice, J.K. and Jowell, R. (1993) *British General Election Study, 1987; Cross-Section Survey*, 2nd edition, UK Data Service, SN: 2568. Available at: http://doi.org/10.5255/UKDA-SN-2568-1 [Accessed 20 February 2020].

Heath, A., Norris, P., Curtice, J.K. and Jowell, R. (1999) *British General Election Study, 1997; Cross-Section Survey*, 2nd edition, UK Data Service, SN: 3887. Available at: http://doi.org/10.5255/UKDA-SN-3887-1 [Accessed 20 February 2020].

Jowell, R., Heath, A. and Curtice, J.K. (1983) *British General Election Study, 1983; Cross-Section Survey*, UK Data Service, SN: 2005. Available at: http://doi.org/10.5255/UKDA-SN-2005-1 [Accessed 20 February 2020].

Jowell, R., Mitchell, J.C., Brand, J.A., Curtice, J.K. and Heath, A. (1993) *British General Election Study, 1992; Cross-Section Survey*, UK Data Service, SN: 2981. Available at: http://doi.org/10.5255/UKDA-SN-2981-1 [Accessed 20 February 2020].

Sanders, D. and Whiteley, P.F. (2014) *British Election Study, 2010: Face-to-Face Survey*, UK Data Service, SN: 7529. Available at: http://doi.org/10.5255/UKDA-SN-7529-1 [Accessed 20 February 2020].

Sanders, D., Whiteley, P.F., Clarke, H. and Stewart, M. (2003) *British General Election Study, 2001; Cross-Section Survey*, UK Data Service, SN: 4619. Available at: http://doi.org/10.5255/UKDA-SN-4619-1 [Accessed 20 February 2020].

112 Bibliography

Sarlvik, B., Crewe, I.M. and Robertson, D.R. (1981) *British Election Study, May 1979; Cross-Section Survey*, UK Data Service, SN: 1533. Available at: http://doi.org/10.5255/UKDA-SN-1533-1 [Accessed 20 February 2020].

Sarlvik, B., Robertson, D.R. and Crewe, I.M. (1981) *British Election Study, February 1974, October 1974, June 1975, May 1979; Panel Survey*, UK Data Service, SN: 1614. Available at: http://doi.org/10.5255/UKDA-SN-1614-1 [Accessed 10 May 2019].

Stewart, M., Whiteley, P.F., Clarke, H. and Sanders, D. (2006) *British Election Study, 2005: Face-to-Face Survey*, UK Data Service, SN: 5494. Available at: http://doi.org/10.5255/UKDA-SN-5494-1 [Accessed 20 February 2020].

University of Essex, Institute for Social and Economic Research (2020) *Understanding Society: Waves 1–9, 2009–2018 and Harmonised BHPS: Waves 1–18, 1991–2009*, 12th edition, UK Data Service, SN: 6614. Available at: http://doi.org/10.5255/UKDA-SN-6614-13 [Accessed 15 July 2020].

References

BBC (1975) Roy Jenkins and Tony Benn Debate: The European Communities Membership Referendum, *BBC Panorama*, 2 June. Available at: www.youtube.com/watch?v=_zBFh6bpcMo [Accessed 10 November 2020].

BBC (2017) Theresa May to Seek General Election on 8 June, *BBC*, 18 April. Available at: www.bbc.co.uk/news/uk-politics-39629603 [Accessed 09 November 2020].

Ben-Nun Bloom, P. and Arikan, G. (2012) A Two-Edged Sword: The Differential Effect of Religious Belief and Religious Social Context on Attitudes towards Democracy, *Political Behaviour*, 34: 249–276.

Ben-Nun Bloom, P. and Arikan, G. (2013) Priming Religious Belief and Religious Social Affects Support for Democracy, *International Journal of Public Opinion Research*, 25: 368–382.

Berger, P.L. (1999) The Desecularization of the World: A Global Overview in Berger, P.L. ed. *The Desecularization of the World: Resurgent Religion and World Politics*, Grand Rapids, William B. Eerdmans Publishing Company: 1–18.

Blair, T. (2011) *A Journey: My Political Life*, New York, Vintage Books.

Bochel, J.M. and Denver, D.T. (1970) Religion and Voting: A Critical Review and a New Analysis, *Political Studies*, 18(2): 205–219.

Boomgaarden, H.G. and Freire, A. (2009) Religion and Euroscepticism: Direct, Indirect or No Effects? *West European Politics*, 32(6): 1240–1265.

Boomgaarden, H.G., Schuck, A., Elenbaas, M. and de Vreese, C.H. (2011) Mapping EU Attitudes: Conceptual and Empirical Dimensions of Euroscepticism and EU Support, *European Union Politics*, 12(2): 241–266.

Brubacker, R. and Cooper, F. (2000) Beyond 'Identity', *Theory and Society*, 29(1): 1–47.

Bruce, S. (2002) *God is dead: Secularization in the West*, Oxford, Blackwell.

Bruce, S. (2018) *Researching Religion: Why We Need Social Science*, Oxford, Oxford University Press.

Bibliography 113

Burgess, K. (2016) Archbishop Will Put His Faith in Staying with EU, *The Times*, 17 May. Available at: www.thetimes.co.uk/article/archbishop-will-put-his-faith-in-staying-with-eu-f29th76j6 [Accessed 10 November 2020].

Caputo, R.K. (2009) Religious Capital and Intergenerational Transmission of Volunteering as Correlates of Civic Engagement, *Nonprofit and Voluntary Sector Quarterly*, 38(6): 983–1002.

Carey, G. (2016) Why I'm Voting for Brexodus: A Revelatory Call to Quit EU from the Former Leader of the Church of England, *Mail Online*, 15 May. Available at: www.dailymail.co.uk/debate/article-3590851/Why-m-voting-Brexodus-revelatory-call-quit-EU-former-leader-Church-England.html [Accessed 11 November 2020].

Carmichael, J.T. and Brulle, R.J. (2017) Elite Cues, Media Coverage, and Public Concern: An Integrated Path Analysis of Public Opinion on Climate Change, 2001–2013, *Environmental Politics*, 26(2): 232–252.

Casanova, J. (2006) Religion, European Secular Identities and European Integration in Byrnes, T.A. and Katzenstein, P.J. eds. *Religion in an Expanding Europe*, Cambridge, Cambridge University Press: 65–92.

Chin, W.W. (1998) Commentary: Issues and Opinion on Structural Equation Modeling, *MIS Quarterly*, 22(1): viii–xvi.

Chrisp, J. and Pearce, N. (2019) Grey Power: Towards a Political Economy of Older Voters in the UK, *The Political Quarterly*, 90(4): 743–756.

Clarke, H.D., Goodwin, M. and Whiteley, P. (2017) *Brexit: Why Britain Voted to Leave the European Union*, Cambridge, Cambridge University Press.

Clements, B. (2015) *Religion and Public Opinion in Britain*, Basingstoke, Palgrave Macmillan.

Collins, P. (2016) Thank Heavens We're All Losing Our Religion, *The Times*, 15 January. Available at: www.thetimes.co.uk/article/thank-heavens-were-all-losing-our-religion-zrxpkr5q0 [Accessed 10 November 2020].

Conservative Party (2017) 2017 General Election Manifesto, *Conservative Party*. Available at: http://ucrel.lancs.ac.uk/wmatrix/ukmanifestos2017/localpdf/Conservatives.pdf [Accessed 10 June 2020].

Corcoran, K. (2016) Now the POPE Wades into Brexit Row: Francis Wants Britain to STAY in EU, *The Express*, 20 January. Available at: www.express.co.uk/news/uk/636585/POPE-against-Brexit-Francis-wants-Britain-to-STAY-in-EU [Accessed 11 November 2020].

Coupland, P.M. (2004) Western Union, 'Spiritual Union' and European Integration, 1948–1951, *Journal of British Studies*, 43(3): 366–394.

Cowley, P. and Kavanagh, D. (2018) *The British General Election of 2017*, Cham, Palgrave Macmillan.

Curtice, J. (2017) The Vote to Leave the EU: Litmus Test or Lightening Rod? in Clery, E., Curtice, J. and Harding, R. eds. *British Social Attitudes 34*, London, NatCen Social Research.

Cutts, D., Goodwin, M., Heath, O. and Surridge, P. (2019) Brexit, the 2019 General Election and the Realignment of British Politics, *The Political Quarterly*, 91(1): 7–23.

Dalton, R.J. (2013) *The Apartisan American*, Thousand Oaks, CQ Press.

Davie, G. (2015) *Religion in Britain: A Persistent Paradox*, 2nd edition, Chichester, Wiley Blackwell.

Bibliography

Davie, G. (2019) European Identity, European Unity and the Christian Tradition in Grebe, M. and Worthen, J. eds. *Church after Brexit: The Church of England, the European Churches and the Future of European Unity*, Leipzig, Evangelische Verlagsanstalt.

de Geus, R.A. and Shorrocks, R. (2020) Where Do Female Conservatives Stand? A Cross-National Analysis of the Issue Positions and Ideological Placement of Female Right-Wing Candidates, *Journal of Women, Politics & Policy*, 41(1): 7–35.

DeHanas, D.N. and Shterin, M. (2018) Religion and the Rise of Populism, *Religion, State and Society*, 46(3): 177–185.

de Vreese, C.H., Azrout, R. and Boomgaarden, H.G. (2019) One Size Fits All? Testing the Dimensional Structure of EU Attitudes in 21 Countries, *International Journal of Public Opinion Research*, 31(2): 195–219.

de Vreese, C.H., Boomgaarden, H.G., Minkenberg, M. and Vliegenthart, R. (2009) Introduction: Religion and the European Union, *West European Politics*, 32(6): 1181–1189.

Dinham, A., Furbey, R. and Lowndes, V. eds. (2009) *Faith in the Public Realm: Controversies, Policies and Practices*, Bristol, Policy Press.

Down, I. and Wilson, C.J. (2013) A Rising Generation of Europeans? Life-cycle and Cohort Effects on Support for Europe, *European Journal of Political Research*, 52(4): 431–456.

Down, I. and Wilson, C.J. (2017) Research Note: A Rising Generation of Europeans? Revisited, *European Journal of Political Research*, 56: 199–214.

Evans, G. and Menon, A. (2017) *Brexit and British Politics*, Cambridge, Polity Press.

Evans, G. and Tilley, J. (2017) *The new politics of class: The political exclusion of the British working class*, Oxford, Oxford University Press.

Fieldhouse, E., Green, J., Evans, G., Mellon, J., Prosser, C., Schmitt, H. and van der Eijk, C. (2020) *Electoral Shocks: The Volatile Voter in a Turbulent World*, Oxford, Oxford University Press.

Finkelstein, D. (2017) Should We Care That Britain's Lost Its Religion? *The Times*, 6 September. Available at: www.thetimes.co.uk/article/should-we-care-that-britain-s-lost-its-religion-v2kx9zqh6 [Accessed 10 November 2020].

Fisher, J. (2020) Party Finance in 2019: Advantage Conservative Party, *Parliamentary Affairs*, 73(Supplement_1): 189–207.

Flanagan, S.C. and Lee, A.R. (2003) The New Politics, Culture Wars, and the Authoritarian-libertarian Value Change in Advanced Industrial Democracies, *Comparative Political Studies*, 36(3): 235–270.

Flood, C. and Soborski, R. (2018) Euroscepticism as Ideology in Leruth, B., Startin, N. and Usherwood, S. eds. *The Routledge Handbook of Euroscepticism*, Abingdon, Routledge: 36–47.

Ford, R. (2019) Immigration: Is Public Opinion Changing, *The UK in a Changing Europe, Brexit and Public Opinion*. Available at: https://ukandeu.ac.uk/wp-content/uploads/2019/01/Public-Opinion-2019-report.pdf [Accessed 11 November 2020].

Ford, R. and Goodwin, M.J. (2014) *Revolt on the Right: Explaining Support for the Radical Right in Britain*, London, Routledge.

Bibliography 115

Ford, R. and Goodwin, M.J. (2017) Britain after Brexit: A Nation Divided, *Journal of Democracy*, 28(1): 17–30.

Fox, S., Hampton, J.M., Muddiman, E. and Taylor, C. (2019) Intergenerational Transmission and Support for EU Membership in the United Kingdom: The Case of Brexit, *European Sociological Review*, 35(3): 380–393.

Fox, S., Muddiman, E., Hampton, J., Kolpinskaya, E. and Evans, C. (forthcoming) The Role of Intergenerational Differences in Religious and Social Capital in Intergenerational Inequality and Conflict, *Sociological Review*.

Fox, S. and Pearce, S. (2018) The Generational Decay of Euroscepticism in the UK and the EU Referendum, *Journal of Elections, Public Opinion and Parties*, 28(1): 19–37.

Gabel, M.J. (1998) *Interests and Integration: Market Liberalization, Public Opinion and European Union*, Ann Arbor, University of Michigan Press.

Geddes, A. (1999) *Britain in the European Union*, Indianapolis, Baseline.

Gifford, C. (2015) Roundtable: Nationalism, Populism and Anglo-British Euroscepticism, *British Politics*, 10: 362–366.

Gifford, C. and Wellings, B. (2018) Referendums and European Integration: The Case of the United Kingdom in Leruth, B., Startin, N. and Usherwood, S. eds. *The Routledge Handbook of Euroscepticism*, Abingdon, Routledge: 268–279.

Goodwin, M.J. and Heath, O. (2016) The 2016 Referendum, Brexit and the Left Behind: An Aggregate-Level Analysis of the Result, *Political Quarterly*, 87(3): 323–332.

Grebe, M. and Worthen, J. (2019) Introduction in Grebe, M. and Worthen, J. eds. *Church after Brexit: The Church of England, the European Churches and the Future of European Unity*, Leipzig, Evangelische Verlagsanstalt.

Guerra, S. (2016) When Catholicism Meets the EU: It's Not Always Euroenthusiasm, *Politiologia*, 1: 25–45.

Halikiopoulou, D. and Vlandas, T. (2018) Voting to Leave: Economic Insecurity and the Brexit Vote in Leruth, B., Startin, N. and Usherwood, S. eds. *The Routledge Handbook of Euroscepticism*, Abingdon, Routledge: 444–455.

Harrop, M. and Miller, W. (1987) *Elections and Voters: A Comparative Introduction*, London, Macmillan International Higher Education.

Heath, A., Taylor, B., Brook, L., and Park, A. (1999) British National Sentiment, *British Journal of Political Science*, 29(1): 155–175.

Henderson, A., Jeffery, C., Wincott, D., and Wyn Jones, R. (2017) How Brexit Was Made in England, *British Journal of Politics and International Relations*, 19(4): 631–646.

Hill, M. (2009) Voices in the Wilderness: The Established Church of England and the European Union, *Religion, State & Society*, 37(1–2): 167–180.

Hobolt, S.B. (2016) The Brexit Vote: A Divided Nation, a Divided Continent, *Journal of European Public Policy*, 23(9): 1259–1277.

Hobolt, S.B. (2018) Brexit and the 2017 UK General Election, *Journal of Common Market Studies*, 56: 39–50.

Hobolt, S.B. and Rodon, T. (2020) Cross-cutting Issues and Electoral Choice: EU Issue Voting in the Aftermath of the Brexit Referendum, *Journal of European Public Policy*, 27(2): 227–245.

Bibliography

Hobolt, S.B., van der Brug, W., de Vreese, C.H., Boomgaarden, H.G. and Hinrichsen, M.C. (2011) Religious Intolerance and Euroscepticism, *European Union Politics*, 12(3): 359–379.

Hooghe, L. and Marks, G. (2005) Calculation, Community and Cues: Public Opinion on European Integration, *European Union Politics*, 6(4): 419–443.

Hornsby-Smith, M.P. (2015) Religion and Politics in the United Kingdom, *Politics and Religion in Europe*, 32(2): 169–194.

Kelloway, E.K. (1995) Structural Equation Modelling in Perspective, *Journal of Organizational Behaviour*, 16(3): 215–224.

Kellstedt, P., McAvoy, G. E. and Stimson, J. A. (1993) Dynamic analysis with latent constructs, *Political Analysis*, 5: 113–150.

Kenny, J., Heath, A.F. and Richards, L. (2019) *Fuzzy Frontiers? Testing the Fluidity of National, Partisan and Brexit Identities in the Aftermath of the 2016 Referendum*, Working paper presented at the 2019 EPOP Annual Conference.

Kiss, Z. and Park, A. (2014) National Identity: Exploring Britishness, *British Social Attitudes 31*, London, NatCen Social Research.

Kolpinskaya, E. and Fox, S. (2019) Praying on Brexit? Unpicking the Effect of Religion on Support for European Union Integration and Membership, *Journal of Common Market Studies*, 57(3): 580–598.

Krouwel, A. and Kutiyshi, Y. (2018) Soft Sceptics and Hard Rejectionists: Identifying Two Types of Eurosceptic Voters in Leruth, B., Startin, N. and Usherwood, S. eds. *The Routledge Handbook of Euroscepticism*, Abingdon, Routledge: 189–203.

Krowel, A. and Abts, K. (2007) Varieties of Euroscepticism and Populist Mobilization: Transforming Attitudes from Mild Euroscepticism to Harsh Eurocynicism, *Acta Politica*, 42(2): 252–270.

Labour Party (2017) 2017 General Election Manifesto, *Labour Party*. Available at: https://labour.org.uk/manifesto-2017/ [Accessed 14 June 2020].

Lam, P. (2002) As the Flocks Gather: How Religion Affects Voluntary Association Participation, *Journal for the Scientific Study of Religion*, 41(3): 405–422.

Leruth, B., Startin, N. and Usherwood, S. (2018) Defining Euroscepticism: From a Broad Concept to a Field of Study in Leruth, B., Startin, N. and Usherwood, S. eds. *The Routledge Handbook of Euroscepticism*, Abingdon, Routledge: 3–10.

Leustean, L.N. ed. (2012) *Representing Religion in the European Union: Does God Matter?* London, Routledge.

Lindberg, L.N. and Scheingold, S.A. (1970) *Europe's Would-be Polity*, Englewood Cliffs, Prentice Hall.

MacColl, A.W. (2016) EU Referendum, *Free Presbyterian Church*. Available at: www.fpchurch.org.uk/2016/06/eu-referendum/ [Accessed 17 July 2020].

Madeley, J. (2003) A Framework for the Comparative Analysis of Church – State Relations in Europe, *West European Politics*, 26(1): 23–50.

Madeley, J. (2007) *Grit or Pearl? The Religious Factor in the Politics of European Integration*, Paper presented at the ECPR 35th Joint Session of Workshops, Helsinki.

Martin, N., Sobolewska, M. and Begum, N. (2019) *Left Out of the Left Behind: Ethnic Minority Support for Brexit*, Working Paper. Available at: www.research

Bibliography 117

gate.net/publication/330730433_Left_Out_of_the_Left_Behind_Ethnic_Minority_Support_for_Brexit [Accessed 10 March 2020].

McAndrew, S. (2017a) Religion and Party Liking: How Members of Different Faith Communities Feel about Different Political Parties, *Religion and the Public Sphere*. Available at: http://eprints.lse.ac.uk/79144/ [Accessed 21 April 2020].

McAndrew, S. (2017b) The EU Referendum, Religion and Identity: Analysing the British Election Study, *Religion and the Public Sphere*. Available at: http://eprints.lse.ac.uk/76503/ [Accessed 21 April 2020].

McAndrew, S. (2020) Belonging, Believing, Behaving, and Brexit: Channels of Religiosity and Religious Identity in Support for Leaving the European Union, *British Journal of Sociology*. Available at: https://doi.org/10.1111/1468-4446.12793 [Accessed 6 November 2020].

McAndrew, S. and Voas, D. (2011) Measuring Religiosity Using Surveys, *Survey Question Bank Topic Overview*, 4. Available at: https://ukdataservice.ac.uk/media/263004/discover_sqb_religion_mcandrew_voas.pdf [Accessed 21 April 2020].

McCrone, D. (2002) Who Do You Say You Are? Making Sense of National Identities in Modern Britain, *Ethnicities*, 2(3): 301–320.

McLaren, L.M. (2003) Anti-immigrant Prejudice in Europe: Contact, Threat Perception, and Preferences for the Exclusion of Migrants, *Social Forces*, 81(3): 909–936.

McLaren, L.M. (2007) Explaining Mass-level Euroscepticism: Identity, Interests, and Institutional Distrust, *Acta Politica*, 42(2–3): 233–251.

McLean, I. and Linsley, B. (2004) *The Church of England and the State: Reforming Establishment for a Multi-faith Britain*, London, New Politics Network.

McLeod, H. (1999) Protestantism and British National Identity, 1815–1945 in Veer, P. and Lehmann, H. eds. *Nation and Religion: Perspectives on Europe and Asia*, Princeton, Princeton University Press: 43–70.

Menon, A. and Fowler, B. (2016) Hard or Soft? The Politics of Brexit, *National Institute Economic Review*, 238: R4–R12.

Minkenberg, M. (2009) Religion and Euroscepticism: Cleavages, Religious Parties and Churches in EU Member States, *West European Politics*, 32(6): 1190–1211.

Mudrov, S.A. (2015) Religion and the European Union: Attitudes of Catholic and Protestant Churches toward European Integration, *Journal of Church and State*, 57(3): 507–528.

Nelsen, B.F. and Guth, J.L. (2003) Religion and Youth Support for the European Union, *Journal of Common Market Studies*, 41: 89–112.

Nelsen, B.F. and Guth, J.L. (2015) *Religion and the Struggle for European Union: Confessional Culture and the Limits of Integration*, Georgetown, Georgetown University Press.

Nelsen, B.F., Guth J.L. and Fraser, C.R. (2001) Does Religion Matter? *European Union Politics*, 2: 191–217.

Nelsen, B.F., Guth, J.L. and Highsmith, B. (2011) Does Religion Still Matter? Religion and Public Attitudes toward Integration in Europe, *Politics and Religion*, 4: 1–26.

Norris, P. and Inglehart, R. (2019) *Cultural Backlash: Trump, Brexit, and Authoritarian Populism*, Cambridge, Cambridge University Press.

Bibliography

Norton, P. (2011) Divided Loyalties: The European Communities Act 1972, *Parliamentary History*. Available at: https://doi.org/10.1111/j.1750-0206.2010.00242.x [Accessed 10 November 2020].

The Observer (2016) Think of the Wider World and Vote to Stay in Europe, *The Observer*, 29 May. Available at: www.theguardian.com/politics/2016/may/28/peace-europe-different-faiths-must-unite [Accessed 10 November 2020].

Park, J.Z. and Smith, C. (2000) 'To Whom Much Has Been Given . . .': Religious Capital and Community Voluntarism among Churchgoing Protestants, *Journal for the Scientific Study of Religion*, 39(3): 272–286.

Peitz, L., Dhont, K. and Seyd, B. (2018) The Psychology of Supranationalism: Its Ideological Correlates and Implications for EU Attitudes and Post-Brexit Preferences, *Political Psychology*, 39(6): 1305–1322.

Philpott, D. and Shah, T.S. (2006) Faith, Freedom, and Federation: The Role of Religious Ideas and Institutions in European Political Convergence in Byrnes, T.A. and Katzenstein, P.J. eds. *Religion in an Expanding Europe*, Cambridge, Cambridge University Press: 34–64.

Pogrund, G. and Maguire, P. (2020) *Left Out: The Inside Story of Labour Under Corbyn*, New York, Vintage Books.

Putnam, R.D. (2000) *Bowling Alone: The Collapse And Revival Of American Community*, New York, Simon & Schuster.

Richards, L., Heath, A. and Elgenius, G. (2019) Remainers Are Nostalgic Too: An Exploration of Attitudes Towards the Past and Brexit Preferences, *British Journal of Sociology*, 71: 74–80.

Ruether, R.R. (1998) *Introducing Redemption in Christian Feminism*, Sheffield, Sheffield Academic Press.

Ryan, B. (2019) A Nation Divided Against Itself? in Grebe, M. and Worthen, J. eds. *Church after Brexit: The Church of England, the European Churches and the Future of European Unity*, Leipzig, Evangelische Verlagsanstalt.

Scherer, M. (2020) Euroscepticism and Protestant Heritage: The Role of Religion on EU Issue Voting, *Politics and Religion*, 13: 119–149.

Seldon, A. (1998) *Major: A Political Life*, London, Phoenix.

Shipman, T. (2017) *Fall Out: A Year of Political Mayhem*, London, William Collins.

Shorrocks, R. (2018) Cohort change in political gender gaps in Europe and Canada: The role of modernization, *Politics & Society*, 46(2): 135–175.

Smith, G. and Woodhead, L. (2018) Religion and Brexit: Populism and the Church of England, *Religion, State and Society*, 46(3): 206–223.

Sobolewska, M. and Ford, R. (2020) *Brexitland: Identity, Diversity and the Reshaping of British Politics*, Cambridge, Cambridge University Press.

Sørensen, C. (2008) *Love Me, Love Me Not: A Typology of Public Euroscepticism*, Sussex European Institute Working Paper 101, Brighton, Sussex European Institute.

Startin, N. (2018) How the Referendum Was Lost: An Analysis of the UK Referendum Campaign on EU Membership in Leruth, B., Startin, N. and Usherwood, S. eds. *The Routledge Handbook of Euroscepticism*, Abingdon, Routledge: 456–467.

Steven, M. (2010) *Christianity and Party Politics: Keeping the Faith*, Abingdon, Routledge.

Taggart, P. and Szczerbiak, A. (2018) Putting Brexit into perspective: the effect of the Eurozone and migration crises and Brexit on Euroscepticism in European states, *Journal of European Public Policy*, 25(8): 1194–1214.

Tilley, J. (2015) 'We Don't Do God'? Religion and Party Choice in Britain, *British Journal of Political Science*, 45(4): 907–927.

Tilley, J., Exley, S. and Heath, A. (2004) Dimensions of British identity, *British Social Attitudes: The 21st Report*. London: SAGE: 147–168.

van der Eijk, C. and Franklin, M. (2009) *Elections and Voters*, London, Palgrave Macmillan.

van der Eijk, C., Franklin, M., Demant, F. and van der Brug, W. (2007) The Endogenous Economy: 'Real' Economic Conditions, Subjective Economic Evaluations and Government Support, *Acta Politica*, 42: 1–22.

Vasilopoulou, S. (2018) Theory, Concepts and Research Design in the Study of Euroscepticism in Leruth, B., Startin, N. and Usherwood, S. eds. *The Routledge Handbook of Euroscepticism*, Abingdon, Routledge: 22–35.

Vincett, G. and Olson, E. (2012) The Religiosity of Young People Growing Up in Poverty in Woodhead, L. and Catto, R. eds. *Religion and Change in Modern Britain*, London, Routledge: 196–202.

Wald, K.D. (1983) *Crosses on the Ballot*, Princeton, Princeton University Press.

Walters, S. (2014) Archbishop of Canterbury Says 'I'm Voting In' as Prime Minister Warns of Defence, Health and Pension Cuts If We Quit EU, *The Daily Mail*, 12 June. Available at: www.dailymail.co.uk/news/article-3637024/Archbishop-Canterbury-says-m-voting-Prime-Minister-warns-defence-health-pension-cuts-quit-EU.html [Accessed 10 November 2020].

Wattenberg, M.P. (2012) *Is voting for young people?: With a new chapter on the 2008 and 2010 election*, New York, Pearson Longman.

Wessels, B. (2007) Discontent and European Identity: Three Types of Euroscepticism, *Acta Politica*, 42(2–3): 287–306.

Wuthnow, R. (2002) Religious Involvement and Status-Bridging Social Capital, *Journal for the Scientific Study of Religion*, 41(4): 669–684.

Wuthnow, R. (2007) *America and the Challenges of Religious Diversity*, Princeton, Princeton University Press.

Wyatt, T. (2016) Rival Campaigns Gear Up to Win Over Christians in EU Referendum Battle, *Church Times*, 4 March. Available at: www.churchtimes.co.uk/articles/2016/4-march/news/uk/rival-campaigns-gear-up-to-win-over-christians-in-eu-referendum-battle [Accessed 10 November 2020].

Index

Note: Page numbers in *italics* indicate a figure and page numbers in **bold** indicate a table on the corresponding page.

affective Euroscepticism (AES) 75–86, 89, 91n3; *see also* utilitarian Euroscepticism (UES)
Amsterdam Treaty 36
Anglicanism 9, 83–84, 86, 89
Anglicans 86–90, 101, 104; affective Euroscepticism (AES) 77; anti-Brexit 14; attitudes towards European integration 8; British adults 61; Catholics and 70; EU membership 46, 59; Eurosceptic Christian 83; Eurosceptic community/Euroscepticism 50, 58, 66, 78; national identities 76; non-Anglicans 28; non-religious and 41; party identification 81; religiously unaffiliated 45; Remainers 101; social conservatism 37; supporting EC membership 37; supporting leaving the EU/supporting Brexit 57, 64, 67–69, 99; vote Conservative 95
Archbishop of Canterbury 56
Archbishop of York 56

Baptists 103; 2016 referendum 9; attitudes towards European integration 8; dissatisfied with EU membership 51; 'non-conformists' 23; non-religious 50; oppose European integration 77; pro-EC 37; religiously active 11; religiously inactive 70; religious participation 61; religious services 68; Remainers 103; socially conservative 88; support for leaving the EC/EU/supporting Brexit 46, 57, 64; voted Conservative 100, 103; in Wales 85
Benn, T. 34
Board of Deputies 56
Boomgaarden, H.G. 20, 73, 108–109
Bradley, I. 56
'Breaking Point' poster 55
Brexit: Anglicans 33; Catholics vote against 11; effect 100–103; 'electoral shock' of 93; 'made in England' 27; opposition 4; probability of supporting *64*, *65*, *67*, *68*; referendum 10, 16, 35, 73, 77–78, 86; religious voters for *102*; support by religious belonging *58*; voter behaviour 12–15; voting before and after 95–103
Brexitland (Ford and Sobolewska) 110
Brexit Party 96
British Christians 55, 94
British Election Study (BES) 4, 10, 34, 37–38, 41, 44, 46–47, 100
British Election Study Internet Panel (BESIP) 73, 79, 84, 101
British Euroscepticism 4, 20, 42, 83, 106
British National Party (BNP) 3, 93
Britishness 27
Brubacker, R. 26

Index 121

Cameron, D. 3, 5, 35, 46, 93
Carey of Clifton, Lord 56
Catholic Church 12, 21, 29–30, 44, 55–56, 88
Catholicism 11, 21–22, 84, 88–89
Catholics 88–90, 96, 99–101; community 29; dissatisfied with EU membership 51; Eurosceptic 70, 86; leaving the EC/EU 46; national identities 77; non-religious 8; opponents of Brexit 68; pro-Brexit 104; pro-EU community 106; pro-Remain Christian communities 57; Remainers 103; Roman 96; supporting Brexit 61, 64, 66–67; supporting Remain 33; supportive of EU membership 65; supportive of European integration 20; vote against Brexit 11; vote Labour 103
Central Europe 45
Christian Democratic Party 15, 95
Christian Democratic Union 15
Christian Democrats 15
Christianity 26, 55
Christians 2; for Britain 55; churches 26; communities 8, 21, 32, 34, 37, 41, 46, 50, 55, 69–70, 77, 94, 96, 104–105; congregations 30; denominations 8, *60*, *97*, *98*; organisations 57; principles 26; religious vote 95; supportive of EC membership 9; tenets 31–32; UK's political parties and 14; voters/vote 15, 24, 36, 88, 95–100, 104; voting 40
Christian Union 15
Church of England 22, 28–30, 34, 39, 55–56, 95–96
Church of Scotland 25, 28, 55
Church of Wales 55
Clements, B. 19
Conservative Eurosceptics 34
Conservative Party 13, 15, 42, 84, 95
Corbyn, J. 94
Covid-19 4

de Geus, R.A. 94
de Vreese, C.H. 20
direct/indirect effects of religion 72–90; structural equation modelling (SEM) 74–75, *75*, 78–87, *81*, *82*; utilitarian 75–78

Eastern Europe 45
elite cues 30–31, 34, 72, 78, 109
England 22, 66, 70, 78–79, 81, *81*, 83–84, 89, 96
Europe 35, 43, 46, 54; identity 22, 44, 83–84, 87; institutions 16, 21, 24–25, 73, 79; integration 2–3, 8, 10, 16, 20–25, 28, 31, 33–34, 36, 39, 43, 55, 66, 69, 73, 75–76, 83, 88–89, 106–107; migration 77; national identity 88; political agenda 42; politics 4; public opinion and electoral events in 5; supranationalism 11; voters' attitudes towards 1; wars 22
European Communities Act (1972) 34–35
European Community (EC) 6, 9–10, 17, 33–35, 37–38, 40, 104
European Union (EU): Great Britain's withdrawal from 1; institutions 10, 76; integrated nature 14; membership 2–5, 9–11, 16–17, 24, 27, 29, 31, 33, 36, 43–47, 50–51, 56, 59, 61, 65–66, 70, 73, 75, 77–79, 84, 87–88, 90, 91n3, 96–100, 106–107; Member States 20, 28, 33, 66; migrants 3; non-discrimination policies 25; referendum 5–6, 13, 79, 99, 103; religion 10; spiritual dimension 26
Euroscepticism 5–15; described 16–17; non-Christian religions and 8; religion 5–15, 20–32, 44–51
Euroscepticism and religion before Brexit 33–53; 1975 referendum 34–42, *39*, *41*; after 1975 42–51
Eurosceptics 16, 20, 22, 34, 36, 46, 63; Labour 34
Evans, G. 1, 42, 100

Fieldhouse, E. 94, 103
First World War 13
Ford, R. 110
Fox, S. 19, 88, 108
Frazer, R. 56
Freire, A. 20, 73, 108–109

Gallagher, P. 56
Gifford, C. 42

Index

Great Britain: Brexit referendum 16; Catholic community 14; Christian communities 21, 34, 37, 94–95, 104–105; Christian congregations 30; Christian 'religious vote' 95; Christian voters 100, 104; economy 35, 54; elections 94–95; entry to the EC 33–34; Euroscepticism in 32; independence 35; membership of the EEC/EU 9, *48*; national identity 27, 35; political parties 14, 54; politics 2–5, 13–15, 16, 34; religion 6, 7; religious communities 50, 68; religious denomination *45*; sovereignty 40; voters 12–15, 44, 93; voting behaviour 103–104; withdrawal from the EU 1, 101
Guth, J.L. 20

Henderson, A. 27
Hilton, A. 55
Hobolt, S.B. 20
House of Commons 35

immigration: British or English national identity and 3; Catholicism 11; Central and Eastern European Member States 51; economy 80; EU membership 31, 43; European integration 93; Euroscepticism 84–85; impact on local economies and communities 11; integration and 44; leave campaigners 54; party identification and attitudes 40, 42, 73, 83, 108; social benefit 94; *see also* mass migration
Independence Referendum 1, 47
indirect effects of religion *see* direct/indirect effects of religion

Janner-Klausner, L. 56
Johnson, B. 5, 92, 94

Kinnock, N. 42
Kolpinskaya, E. 88, 108

Labour Party 42, 77, 94, 96, 110
Lam, P. 19
Leavers 3, 9, 54–55; *see also* Remainers

left/right 73, 77–78, 80, 93, 110
Leruth, B. 2
Liberal Democrats 13–15, 47, 77–78, 96, 99–100, 103–104, 110
Liberal Party 96
Lisbon Treaty 26, 36, 43

Maastricht Treaty 36, 42
Major, J. 42
Marr, A. 1
mass migration 3, 24, 34, 90; *see also* immigration
May, T. 92
McAndrew, S. 31, 55, 73, 94, 108–109
McMahon, T. 56
Menon, A. 1, 42
Methodists 62, 100, 103–104; 2016 referendum 9; Calvinist 96; Conservative support 14; EC membership 9, 37–38; EU membership 50–51; European integration 8, 77; Euroscepticism/Eurosceptics 41, 46, 78, 103; religiously inactive 70; religious participation 61; Remainers 103; socially conservative 11, 88; support for Liberal Democrats and Catholics 104; supporting Brexit 57, 65, 68
middle-class 2
Minkenberg, M. 20
Murphy-O'Connor, C. 56
Muslim Council of Britain 56

national identity 75–77, 93, 106; Brexit 4; Christianity 26; Church of England 22; English/British/Scottish/Welsh/European 3, 8, 10–11, 22, 25–28, 35–37, 51–52, 55, 63, 69, 80, 82–84, 87–88, 99, 110; European integration 28; Euroscepticism 63, 73, 101, 104; free church Protestants 23; political and social ideologies and 34; political values and 10; religion and 26–29, 63, 75; religious communities 28; social conservatism/conservatives and 14, 28, 73, 83, 101; traditional 44, 55; 'unique national identity' 35
Nelsen, B.F. 20
New Labour 43

non-Christian faiths/religions 8, 26
non-conformists 13, 23, 95–96
Norton, P. 34

Orthodox Christians 20

party identification 29–30, 78, 80
Pius XII, Pope 39
Plaid Cymru 80–81, 85
political ideology 21, 23–26, 72, 83, 106, 108–109
political institutions 1, 3, 12, 21–23, 77, 89
post-Christian Europe 26
Powell, E. 34–35
Presbyterian Church of Scotland 95
Presbyterianism 84, 86
Presbyterians 76–78, 83–84, 86–90, 101, 104; EU membership 9, 50–51; European integration 8, 66; opponents of Brexit 68; pro-EU country 58; religiously inactive 61; as Scottish 28; supported Remain 33; support for leaving the EC/EU 46; supporting Brexit 57, 65, 99; vote Conservative 95
Protestantism 21–22, 28, 87–89
Protestants 8, 20, 22, 37, 65, 76–77, 87–88, 96, 106–107

'red wall' constituencies 94
regression analysis 75; demographic and socio-economic characteristics 63; Euroscepticism *74*; Presbyterians 65; religion and the Brexit referendum *64*, 64–68, *65*, *67*, *68*; religious community 40, 67; religious effects 47; religious identification 40
religion: 1975 referendum and 34–42, *39*, *41*; British politics and 1–15; described 17–20; European Union (EU) 10; Euroscepticism 5–15, 9, 20–32, **86**; Great Britain 6, 7; hypothesised relationship between *80*; identity 26–29; non-Christian 8; structural equation modelling (SEM) 74–75, *75*
religion and Brexit referendum 54–71; regression analyses *64*, 64–68, *65*,

67, *68*; religious effects 62–64; vote choice in 2016 referendum 57–62
religion and party politics in Brexit 92–105; Brexit effect 100–103; Christian vote 95–100; EU membership 96–100; voting before and after Brexit 95–103
religious behaviour 19–20, 30–31, **60**, 65
religious beliefs 19–20, 31–32, 66, 71n1
religious belonging 19, 44–51; 1975 referendum *41*; history of political and religious institutions 21–23; party identification 29–30; political ideology 23–26; religion and national identity 26–29
religious denomination: 1975 referendum by *36*; Great Britain *45*
religious effects 10, 38, 62–64
religious identity 4, 8–13, 21, 59, 71, 86, 89
religious institutions 21–23, 25, 34, 55
religious voters 39
Remainers 3, 9, 54–55, 101, 103; *see also* Leavers
Rich, D. 56
Roman Catholics *see* Catholics

Sadgrove, M. 55
Scotland 47, 66, 78–81, *82*, 83–84, 86, 89, 96
Scottish National Party (SNP) 47, 78, 80–81, 96, 99, 101, 104
Shorrocks, R. 94
Singh, J. 56
Single European Act 16
Smith, G. 30
Sobolewska, M. 110
social capital 30–31, 78
social conservatism 24, 37, 44, 75, 77, 83–84, 87, 89, 94, 101
Social Democrats 42
social identities 2, 18–19
statistical significance 37–38
Steven, M. 95
structural equation modelling (SEM) 12, 74–75, *75*, 78–87, 90, 91n3
supranationalism 11, 23, 76, 106

Ten Commandments 23
Thatcher, M. 42, 99

Tilley, J. 94, 100
Tory Party 12

UK Parliament 35, 79
United Kingdom Household Longitudinal Surveys (UKHLS) 4, 6, 57, 59, 63–64, 71nn1–2
United Kingdom Independence Party (UKIP) 3, 43, 78, 93, 96
United States 54
utilitarian: AES and 89; (in)direct effects of religion 75–78
utilitarian Euroscepticism (UES) 77–84, 86, 89–90, 91n3; *see also* affective Euroscepticism (AES)

Vatican 21
Versi, M. 56
voter behaviour: Brexit 12–15, 101; Europe 5; in Great Britain 5, 12–15; post-referendum 94; public opinion and 101

Wales 22, 66, 70, 78–81, *82*, 83–84, 89
Wellings, B. 42
Williams, R. 56
Wilson, H. 35
Woodhead, L. 30
working-class 2–3, 14, 43, 45, 93, 96, 100, 110